WHO WAS FIRST?

WHO WAS FIRST?

Discovering the Americas

—by—

Russell Freedman

CLARION BOOKS ❦ NEW YORK

To Jim and Carol,
my fellow explorers

Clarion Books
a Houghton Mifflin Company imprint
215 Park Avenue South, New York, NY 10003
Copyright © 2007 by Russell Freedman

The text was set in 13-point Berkeley.
Book design by Trish Parcell Watts
Maps by Kayley LeFaiver

www.clarionbooks.com

Manufactured in China.

Library of Congress Cataloging-in-Publication Data
Freedman, Russell.
Who was first? : discovering the Americas / by Russell Freedman.
p. cm.
Includes bibliographical references and index.
ISBN: 978-0-618-66391-0
1. Explorers—America—Biography—Juvenile literature. 2. America—Discovery
and exploration—Juvenile literature. 3. America—Discovery and exploration—
Pre-Columbian—Juvenile literature. I. Title.
E101.F885 2007
970.01 22
2006102485

WKT 10 9 8 7 6 5 4 3 2 1

Frontispiece: *Christopher Columbus lands in the New World. This engraving,
by Alphonse Bigot, appeared in* An Illuminated History of North America,
from the Earliest Period to the Present Time, *by John Frost, published in 1856.*

CONTENTS

BEFORE COLUMBUS

OR A LONG TIME, most people believed that Christopher Columbus was the first explorer to "discover" America—the first to make a successful round-trip voyage across the Atlantic. But in recent years, as new evidence has come to light, our understanding of history has changed. We now know that Columbus was among the last explorers to reach the Americas, not the first.

Five hundred years before Columbus, a daring band of Vikings led by Leif Eriksson set foot in North America and established a settlement. And long before that, some scholars say, the Americas were visited by seafaring travelers from China, and possibly by visitors from Africa and even Ice Age Europe.

A popular legend suggests an additional event: According to an ancient manuscript, in the sixth century a band of Irish monks led by Saint Brendan sailed an ox-hide boat westward in search of new lands. After seven years they returned home and reported that they had discovered a land covered with luxuriant vegetation, believed by some people today to have been Newfoundland.

All along, of course, the two continents we now call North and South America had already been "discovered." Before European explorers arrived, the Americas were home to tens of millions of native peoples. While the Native American groups differed greatly from one another, they all performed rituals and ceremonies, songs and dances, that brought to mind and heart memories of the ancestors who had come before them and given them their place on Earth.

Who were the ancestors of those Native Americans? Where did they come from, when did they arrive in the Americas, and how did they make their epic journeys?

As we dig deeper and deeper into the past, we find that the Americas have always been lands of immigrants, lands that have been "discovered" time and again by different peoples coming from different parts of the world over the course of countless generations—going far back to the prehistoric past, when a band of Stone Age hunters first set foot in what truly was an unexplored New World.

A Viking ship heads out into the open sea.
Undated lithograph by J. Hofdijk.

The ships of Columbus: the Niña, Pinta, *and* Santa María. *An illustration from* History of the United States and Its People, *by Edward Eggleston, published in 1888.*

Chapter One

ADMIRAL OF THE OCEAN SEA

CHRISTOPHER COLUMBUS was having trouble with his crew. His fleet of three small sailing ships had left the Canary Islands nearly three weeks earlier, heading west across the uncharted Ocean Sea, as the Atlantic was known. He had expected to reach China or Japan by now, but there was still no sign of land.

None of the sailors had ever been so long away from the sight of land, and as the days passed, they grew increasingly restless and fearful. The Ocean Sea was also known as the Sea of Darkness. Hideous monsters were said to lurk beneath the waves—venomous sea serpents and giant crabs that could rise up from the deep and crush a ship along with its crew. And if the Earth was flat, as many of the men believed, then they might fall off the edge of the world and plunge into that fiery abyss where the sun sets in the west. What's more, Columbus

was a foreigner—a red-headed Italian commanding a crew of tough seafaring Spaniards—and that meant he couldn't be trusted.

Finally, the men demanded that Columbus turn back and head for home. When he refused, some of the sailors whispered together of mutiny. They wanted to kill the admiral by throwing him overboard. But, for the moment, the crisis passed. Columbus managed to calm his men and persuade them to be patient a while longer.

"I am having serious trouble with the crew . . . complaining that they will never be able to return home," he wrote in his journal. "They have said that it is insanity and suicidal on their part to risk their lives following the

Sea monsters as depicted by the German cartographer Sebastian Münster, whose Cosmographia, *published in 1544, was the earliest German description of the world and one of the most popular books of the sixteenth century.*

madness of a foreigner. . . . I am told by a few trusted men (and these are few in number!) that if I persist in going onward, the best course of action will be to throw me into the sea some night."

All along, Columbus had been keeping two sets of logs. One, which he kept secretly and showed to no one, was accurate, recording the distance really sailed each day. The other log, which he showed to his crew, hoping to reassure them that they were nowhere near the edge of the world, deliberately underestimated the miles they had covered since leaving Spain.

They sailed on for another two weeks and still saw nothing. There were more rumblings of protest and complaint from the crew; the men seemed willing to endure no more. On October 10, Columbus announced that he would give a fine silk coat to the man who first sighted land. The sailors greeted that offer with glum silence. What good was a silk coat in the middle of the Sea of Darkness?

Later that day, Columbus spotted a flock of birds flying toward the southwest—a sign that land was close. He ordered his ships to follow the birds.

The next night, the moon rose in the east shortly before midnight. About two hours later, at two A.M. on October 12, a sailor on one of Columbus's ships, the *Pinta,* saw a white stretch of beach, shouted, "Land! Land!" and fired a cannon. At dawn, the three ships dropped anchor in the calm blue waters just offshore. They had arrived at an island in what we now call the Bahamas.

Excited crew members crowded the decks. They saw people standing on the beach, waiting to greet them. The natives had no weapons other than wooden fishing spears, and they were practically naked. Who were these people? And what place was this?

Columbus supposed that his fleet had landed on one of the many islands that Marco Polo had reported lay just off the coast of Asia. They must have reached the Indies, he thought—islands near India known today as the East

At their first sight of land after weeks at sea, Columbus's crew fall thankfully at his feet. An 1892 illustration by M. F. Tobin.

Indies. So he decided that those people on the beach must be "Indians," the name by which they have been known ever since. China and Japan, he believed, lay a bit farther to the north.

Portrait of a man believed to be Christopher Columbus by the Italian painter Sebastiano del Piombo (1485–1547). No authentic contemporary portrait of Columbus has ever been found. His face remains a mystery.

Though Christopher Columbus was an Italian born in Genoa, he had lived for years in Portugal, where he worked as a bookseller, a mapmaker, and a sailor. He had sailed on Portuguese ships as far as Iceland in the North Atlantic and down the coast of Africa in the South Atlantic. During his days at sea, he read books on history, geography, and travel.

Like most educated people at the time, Columbus believed that the Earth was round—not flat, as some ignorant folks still insisted. The Ocean Sea was seen as a great expanse of water surrounding the land mass of Eurasia, which stretched from Europe in the west to China and Japan in the far distant east. If a ship left the coast of Europe, sailed west toward the setting sun, and circled the globe, it would reach the shores of Asia—or so Columbus thought.

In the past, European explorers and traders had taken the overland route to the Far East, with its precious silks and spices. They traveled for months by horse and camel along the Silk Road, an ancient caravan trail that crossed deserts and climbed dizzying mountain peaks. Marco Polo had followed the Silk Road on his famous journey to China two centuries earlier. But recently, this land route to Asia, controlled in part by the Turks, had been closed to Europeans. And in any case, Columbus was convinced that he could find an easier and faster route to Asia by sailing west across the Ocean Sea.

There were plenty of stories circulating in those years about the possibility of sailing directly from Europe to Asia, an idea first suggested by the ancient Greeks. Columbus owned a book called *Imago Mundi,* or *Image of the World,* by a French scholar, Pierre d'Ailly, who argued that the Ocean Sea wasn't as wide as it seemed and that a ship driven by favorable winds could cross it in a few days. Next to that passage in the margin of the book, Columbus had written: "There is no reason to think that the ocean covers half the earth."

In 1484, he proposed his bold scheme of sailing west to China to King John II of Portugal, a monarch who had paid much attention to the discovery of new lands. Portugal was Europe's leading maritime power. Portuguese explorers in search of slaves, ivory, and gold had already discovered rich kingdoms and colossal rivers in western Africa and would soon reach the Cape of Good Hope at Africa's southern tip. From there, they would be able to sail across the Indian Ocean to the famed Spice Islands of southeast Asia.

King John listened to what Columbus had to say, then submitted the Italian sailor's plan to a committee of mapmakers, astronomers, and geographers. The distinguished experts declared that Asia must be much farther away than Columbus thought. They said that no expedition could be fitted out with enough food and water to sail across such an enormous expanse of sea.

Rejected by the Portuguese king, Columbus decided to approach King Ferdinand and Queen Isabella of Spain, a country he had never before visited. Well-connected friends gave him letters of introduction to the inner circle of the Spanish royal court. Ferdinand and Isabella seemed curious about the route to Asia that Columbus proposed. Like King John, they appointed a committee of inquiry to consider the matter, but those experts came to the same negative conclusion: Columbus's claim about the distance to China and the ease of sailing there could not possibly be true.

Columbus kneels before Queen Isabella at the Spanish royal court in this nineteenth-century French lithograph.

Columbus persisted. He talked at length to members of the Spanish court and convinced some of them, but not Ferdinand and Isabella, who twice rejected his appeal for ships. Finally, angry and impatient after six discouraging years in Spain, he threatened to seek support from the king of France. Columbus actually set out for France, riding a mule down a dusty Spanish road.

With that, royal advisers persuaded Ferdinand and Isabella to change their minds. If the French king sponsored Columbus, and his expedition turned out to be a success, then the Spanish monarchs would be embarrassed. They would be criticized in Spain. Let Columbus risk his life, the advisers said. Let him seek out "the grandeurs and secrets of the universe." If he succeeded, Spain would win much glory and would overcome the Portuguese lead in the race to exploit the riches of Asia.

And so Ferdinand and Isabella decided to take a chance. They dispatched a messenger to intercept Columbus on the road and bring him back to court. They were ready to grant him a hereditary title, Admiral of the Ocean Sea, and the right to a tenth of any riches—pearls, gold, silver, silks, spices—that he brought back from his voyage. And they agreed to supply two ships for his expedition. Columbus himself raised the money to hire a third ship.

A half hour before sunrise on August 3, 1492, the *Niña*, the *Pinta*, and the *Santa María* sailed from the port of Palos, Spain, carrying some ninety crew members in all.

They were small, lightweight ships called caravels, swift and maneuverable, each with three masts, their white sails with big red crosses billowing before the wind. They had on board food that would last—salted cod, bacon, and biscuits, along with flour, wine, olive oil, and plenty of water, enough for a year. In his small cabin, Columbus kept several hourglasses to mark the passage of time, a compass, and an astrolabe, an instrument for calculating latitude by observing the movement of the sun.

The little fleet stopped for repairs at La Gomera in the Canary Islands, a Spanish possession off the coast of Morocco. On September 6, after praying at the parish

A priest blesses Columbus and his men as they prepare to sail into the unknown Ocean Sea. An 1892 engraving by Amadeo Roca Gisbert.

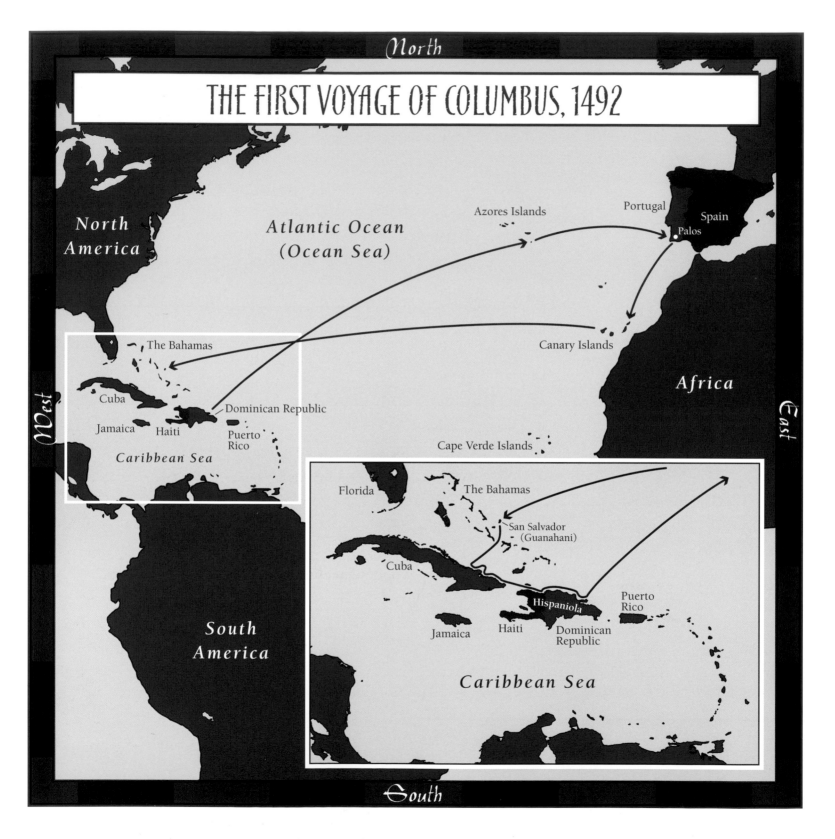

church of San Sebastian (which still looks out over the ocean today), Columbus and his three ships set sail again, heading due west, moving now through the unknown waters of the Ocean Sea. Five weeks later, on October 12, his worried crew finally sighted land.

Columbus called the place where they landed San Salvador. It was the first of many Caribbean islands that he would name. The natives who greeted him called their island Guanahani. They themselves were a people known as the Tainos, the largest group of natives inhabiting the islands of what we today call the West Indies.

Columbus tells us a few things about these now-extinct people. He was impressed by their good looks and apparent robust health. "They are very well-built people, with handsome bodies and very fine faces," he wrote in his log. "Their eyes are large and very pretty. . . . These are tall people and their legs, with no exceptions, are quite straight, and none of them has a paunch." Many of the Tainos had painted their faces or their whole bodies black or white or red. And as Columbus and his men noticed right away, some of them wore gold earrings and nose rings. They offered gifts to the European visitors—parrots, wooden javelins, and balls of cotton thread.

From San Salvador, Columbus sailed on to several other islands, still believing that he was close to Japan, "because all my globes and world maps seem to indicate that the island of Japan is in this vicinity." He stopped at Cuba and at Hispaniola (the island that today includes Haiti and the Dominican Republic). And he wrote enthusiastically in his journal of the lush tropical beauty of the islands, the sweet singing of birds "that might make a man wish never to leave here," and the hospitality of the people: "They gave my men bread and fish and whatever they had." And later, "They brought us all they had in this world, knowing what I wanted, and they did it so generously and willingly that it was wonderful."

The Tainos lived in large, airy wooden houses with palm roofs. They slept in cotton hammocks, sat on wooden chairs carved in elaborate animal shapes, and kept small barkless dogs and tame birds as pets. They were skilled farmers, fishermen, and boat builders who traveled from island to island in long, brightly painted canoes carved from tree trunks, each of which carried as many as 150 people.

The Tainos lived in wooden houses, usually arranged around a central plaza. They slept in cotton hammocks. These drawings first appeared in Natural History of the West Indies, *by Gonzalo Fernández de Oviedo y Valdés, published in Spain in 1526.*

They told Columbus that they called themselves Tainos, a word meaning "good," to distinguish themselves from the "bad" Caribs, their fierce, warlike neighbors who raided Taino villages, carried off their girls as brides, and, the Tainos insisted, ate human flesh. To fend off Carib attacks, the Tainos painted themselves red and fought back with clubs, bows and arrows, and spears propelled by throwing sticks.

The Tainos themselves were not warlike, Columbus reported to his monarchs: "They are an affectionate people, free from avarice and agreeable to everything. I certify to Your Highnesses that in all the world I do not believe there is a better people or a better country. They love their neighbors as themselves, and they have the softest and gentlest voices in the world and are always smiling."

A village chief gave Columbus a mask with golden eyes and large ears of gold. And the Spaniards were already aware that many of the Tainos wore gold jewelry. They kept asking where the gold came from. After much searching, they found a river on the island of Hispaniola where "the sand was full of gold, and in such quantity, that it is wonderful. . . . I named this *el Rio del Oro*" (the River of Gold).

Columbus built a small fort nearby and left thirty-nine men behind to collect gold samples and await the next Spanish expedition. Still believing that he had discovered unknown islands near the shores of Asia, he sailed back to Spain with some gold from Hispaniola and with ten Indians he had kidnapped so he could train them as

A wooden Taino chair, carved in an animal shape and inlaid with gold. From Mitología y artes prehispánicas de las Antillas, *by Jose J. Arrom, 1975.*

interpreters and exhibit them at the royal court. One of
the Indians died at sea.

He returned to a triumphant welcome. It was said that
when Ferdinand and Isabella received him at their court
in Barcelona, "there were tears in the royal eyes." They
greeted Columbus as a hero, inviting him to ride with
them in royal processions.

A second voyage was planned. This time, the monarchs gave Columbus seventeen ships, with about fifteen
hundred men and a few women to colonize the islands.

*Columbus stands before the king and queen of Spain,
displaying gold jewelry and Indians he has brought
from the New World. An 1893 lithograph.*

He was instructed to continue his explorations, establish gold mines, install settlers, develop trade with the Indians, and convert them to Christianity.

Columbus returned to Hispaniola in the fall of 1493. He hoped to find huge amounts of gold on the island. But the mines yielded much less gold than expected, and the European crops planted by the settlers wilted in the tropical climate. Some settlers began to lord it over the Indians, stealing their possessions, abducting their wives, and seizing captives to be shipped to Spain and sold as slaves. Thousands of Tainos fled to the mountains to escape capture. Others, vowing to avenge themselves, attacked any small groups of Spaniards they found and set fire to their huts.

While Columbus was a courageous and enterprising mariner, he proved to be a poor governor, unable to control the greed of his followers. In 1496, he was called back to Spain to answer complaints about his management of the colony. When he appeared at court before Ferdinand and Isabella, he found that the king and queen were still willing to support his explorations. Columbus gave them a "good sample of gold . . . and many masks, with eyes and ears of gold, and many parrots." He also presented to the monarchs "Diego," the brother of a Taino chief, who was wearing a heavy gold collar. These hints that more gold might be forthcoming encouraged Ferdinand and Isabella to send Columbus back to the Indies, this time with eight ships.

When he returned to Hispaniola on his third voyage, in 1498, he found the island in turmoil, torn by rivalries and disagreements among the settlers. Many colonists, unable to make a living from the gold mines or by farming, were clamoring to return to Spain. Others, rivals of Columbus who wanted to gain control of the colony, rebelled against his rule. When word of the conflict reached Spain, the king and queen sent an emissary, Francisco de Bobadilla, to investigate the uprising and take charge of the government.

Columbus, it seems, made the mistake of arguing with the royal emissary and challenging his credentials. He was promptly arrested and with his two brothers was shipped back to Spain to face charges of wrongdoing. "Bobadilla sent me here in chains," he wrote to Ferdinand and Isabella when he landed in Spain. "I swear that I do

Columbus is shipped back to Spain in chains. A 1905 engraving.

not know, nor can I think why." Though Columbus was quickly pardoned by the Spanish monarchs, who felt he had been treated too harshly, he was stripped of his right to govern the islands he had discovered, and he lost his title as Admiral of the Ocean Sea.

Even so, he was allowed to make one more voyage, sailing across the Caribbean and exploring the coast of Central America. This final expedition was cursed by bad luck. Two of Columbus's ships became so infested with termites, they sank. When he headed back to Spain, he had to beach his remaining ships at St. Ann's Bay in Jamaica, where he was marooned for a year before being rescued in the fall of 1504. He returned to Spain an ill and disappointed man.

Spanish colonists, meanwhile, had been settling in Hispaniola, Cuba, Puerto Rico, Jamaica, and other islands in the West Indies. The local Indians were put to work as forced laborers in the goldfields or on Spanish ranches. Those who resisted were killed, sometimes with terrible brutality, or were shipped to Spain to be sold as slaves. Spanish missionaries denounced this mistreatment, but with little effect. "I have seen the greatest cruelty and inhumanity practiced on these gentle and peace-loving [native peoples]," Father Bartolomé de Las Casas would say a half century later, "without any reason except for insatiable greed, thirst, and hunger for gold."

As the number of Spanish colonists increased, the native population of the West Indies quickly declined. Tens of thousands of native people were worked to death or died of smallpox, measles, and other European dis-

eases to which they had no immunity. As the Tainos died off, the colonists brought in black slaves from Africa to labor on ranches and in the spreading sugar-cane fields.

Within fifty years, the Tainos had ceased to exist as a distinct race of people. A few Taino words survive today in Spanish and even in English, including *hammock, canoe, hurricane, savannah, barbecue,* and *cannibal.*

Columbus died in a Spanish monastery on May 20, 1506, at the age of fifty-seven, still believing that he had found a new route to Asia, and that China and Japan lay just beyond the islands he had explored. By then, other explorers were following the sea route pioneered by the Admiral of the Ocean Sea, and Europeans were already speaking of Columbus's discoveries as a "New World."

Indians worked as forced laborers in the goldfields of the New World.

The first map of the world to show these newly discovered lands across the Ocean Sea appeared in 1507, a year after Christopher Columbus's death. The mapmaker, Martin Waldseemüller, named the New World "America," after Amerigo Vespucci, an Italian who had explored the coastline of South America and was the first to realize that it was a separate continent, not part of Asia.

Columbus, however, was given credit for "discovering" America. His voyages were significant because they were the first to become widely known in Europe. They opened a pathway from the Old World to the New, paving the way for the European conquest and colonization of the Americas, changing life forever on both sides of the Atlantic.

Columbus on his deathbed, May 20, 1506. Lithograph published in 1893.

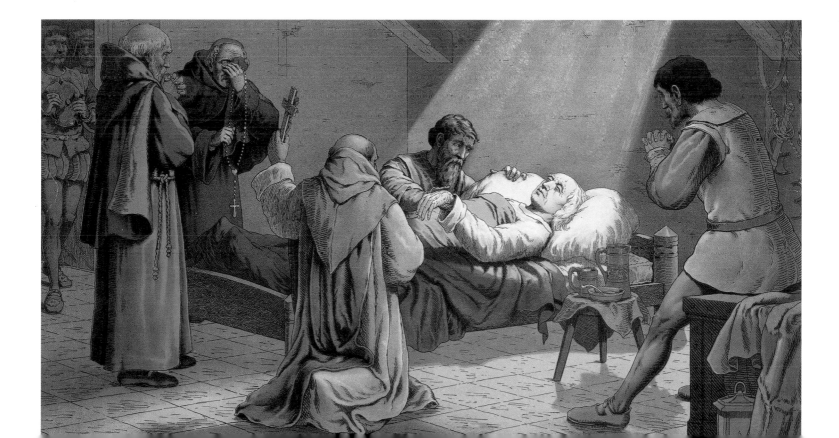

Chapter Two

DID CHINA DISCOVER AMERICA?

O N A SPRING MORNING in the year 1421, a mighty Chinese armada, one of the largest fleets the world had ever seen, set sail for the far corners of the Earth. To ensure a safe passage and success on the journey, the ships' captains and crews placed themselves in the hands of the gods, burning incense and chanting prayers:

> Let the dark water dragons go down into the sea and leave us free from calamity . . .
> That our sails may meet favorable winds
> That the sea lanes be peaceful and secure
> That our coming and going be auspicious
> That gold, pearls, wealth, and valuables fill our ships with glory
> That crossing the seas, coming and going, we follow the correct route. . . .

The Travels of Zheng He, *an oil painting by Qi Pang, commissioned by the Ventura County Maritime Museum for its 2005–2006 exhibit* "When China Ruled the Seas: The Treasure Fleet of the Ming Dynasty, 1405–1433." *No contemporary portrait of Zheng He is known to exist. This modern artist's impression is based on written descriptions from the fifteenth century.*

Exactly how far did those ships travel as they crossed the seas? Is it possible that seafaring explorers from China set foot in America seventy-one years before Columbus?

China at the time was the world's greatest naval power. Its shipyards regularly turned out some of the biggest wooden sailing vessels ever built. The Chinese called them *bao chuan*, treasure ships, because of the vast amount of precious goods they carried in their enormous holds.

The actual size of these ships is unknown. Some historical records suggest that the largest treasure ships, with as

No one knows exactly what Zheng He's treasure ships looked like. This four-foot model, completed in 2005, represents a scholarly consensus. It was researched and built by members of the Ventura County Maritime Museum Model Guild: William Conroy, Sergio Aragones, Richard Welton, and David Andersen.

many as nine masts and twelve sails, were each more than four hundred feet long and carried a crew of several hundred men. Columbus's biggest ship, the *Santa María,* was eighty-five feet long and had a crew of forty.

As the Chinese fleet set sail in 1421, the brightly decorated treasure ships rode the waves at the center of the armada, their silk sails unfurled like red clouds against the sky. Glaring serpents' eyes painted on the ships' prows were meant to frighten away evil spirits. Gong Zhen, an official who sailed with the fleet, described the treasure ships as "lofty and majestic in physical form and appearance . . . incomparably gigantic." They were escorted by scores of smaller support vessels—supply ships; water tankers; transports for cavalry horses; swift, maneuverable patrol boats; and heavily armed warships meant to terrorize pirates.

All together, the great armada included some 250 oceangoing vessels with perhaps 28,000 crew members, including astrologers to forecast the weather, astronomers to study the stars, ship-repair specialists, medical officers, and interpreters for Arabic and other languages. Communication among the ships was accomplished by an elaborate system of signal flags, bells, drums, gongs, and lanterns. Drums loud enough to be heard by neighboring ships warned of approaching storms. Lanterns conveyed signals at night. Carrier pigeons were dispatched for long-range communication.

The fleet's commander, Admiral Zheng He, traveled in his sea cabin high above the stern of his flagship. A powerful figure who was said to be over seven feet tall and have a stride like a tiger's and a voice "as loud as a huge bell," he wore his formal admiral's uniform, a long red silk robe and a tall black hat that made him appear even taller. His eyes, according to a court official, "sparkled like light on a fast-moving river," evidence of his energy and vitality.

Under Admiral Zheng's command, Chinese treasure fleets made seven epic voyages between 1405 and 1433. Loaded with expensive porcelains, lacquerware, and silks, gigantic junks sailed throughout the China Seas and the Indian Ocean, calling at ports in Sumatra, Ceylon, and India; visiting the Persian Gulf, the Arabian Peninsula, and the distant shores of Africa; and trading with Indian, Arab, and African merchants. The ships returned home carrying spices, ivory, medicines, and precious stones destined for the Chinese Imperial Court, and with exotic creatures such as zebras and giraffes, which were presented ceremoniously to the delighted emperor.

Although each treasure ship was equipped with as many as twenty-four cast-iron cannons, which had a range of eight or nine hundred feet, they were not considered fighting ships. Their valuable cargoes were protected from roving bands of pirates by warships armed with an array of incendiary and explosive weapons. "Sky-flying tubes" delivered sprays of gunpowder and flaming bits of paper to set fire to the enemy's sails and cripple their ships. "Gunpowder buckets" and "fire bricks" were explosive grenades soaked in poison. Other grenades were packed with metal pellets that could maim and kill enemy sailors, or with foul-smelling or smoke-producing

Opposite: *A silk scroll created by an unknown artist in 1414 depicts the giraffe, with its attendant, that was sent from Africa to the Chinese Imperial Court. Calligraphy at the top of the scroll reads in part:* Gentle is this animal that in all antiquity has been sent but once.

chemicals intended to frighten and blind the enemy. During one fierce battle in the Strait of Malacca, Zheng He's forces ambushed a notorious pirate fleet and, one by one, burned ten of the pirates' warships and captured seven others.

These voyages are well-documented history, and they inspired a legend. Admiral Zheng was also known by the name of Sin-Bao. Sailors who served with him would gather after their long journeys and spin tales of their adventures across the seas. As the tales were told and retold over the years, Zheng's seven expeditions became legendary, even in the West, as the seven voyages of Sinbad the Sailor. "I have seen oceans where the sun rises," the tales begin, "and have trod atolls that are like giants' rings fallen from the sky."

Scholars agree that Zheng He's treasure ships did in fact sail down the east coast of Africa, at least as far as present-day Kenya. The ships might have continued around the southern tip of Africa, and from there sailed across the Atlantic to America. The Chinese had accurate magnetic compasses (a Chinese invention) to help them navigate, and their ships were capable of sailing some of the world's roughest seas. But did they really venture beyond Africa? This is where documented history gives way to speculation and guesswork.

৯

Gavin Menzies, a retired British Navy submarine commander and a self-taught historian, believes that Chinese mariners reached the Americas seven decades before

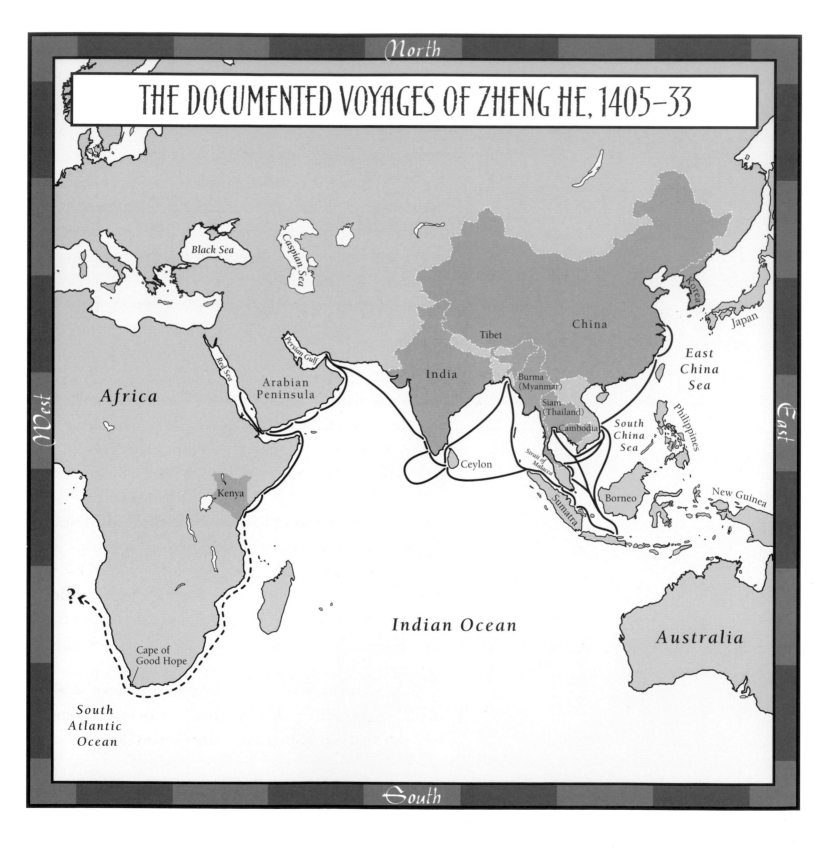

THE DOCUMENTED VOYAGES OF ZHENG HE, 1405–33

North

West

East

South

Black Sea

Caspian Sea

Red Sea

Persian Gulf

Arabian Peninsula

Africa

Tibet

China

India

Burma (Myanmar)

Siam (Thailand)

Cambodia

Korea

Japan

East China Sea

South China Sea

Philippines

Ceylon

Strait of Malacca

Sumatra

Borneo

New Guinea

Kenya

Indian Ocean

Australia

Cape of Good Hope

South Atlantic Ocean

Columbus and circumnavigated the globe a century before Magellan. Challenging accepted history, Menzies argues that ships commanded by Zheng He ventured far beyond the Indian Ocean during their voyage of 1421. Rounding the Cape of Good Hope at Africa's southern tip, the treasure fleets went on to cross the Atlantic and sail around the world, mapping the coasts of North and South America, establishing colonies in Rhode Island, Puerto Rico, Mexico, Peru, California, and British Columbia, even reaching Antarctica and the Arctic before sailing back to China.

No written record describing such a remarkable voyage is known to exist. To support his theory, Menzies cites mysterious carved stones and ancient structures found in the Americas, what might be the buried remains of shipwrecks, and early European maps that appear to show parts of the world not known to European explorers at the time they were drawn. He describes this and other evidence in his controversial book *1421: The Year China Discovered America*.

Menzies argues that charts made by the Chinese during their round-the-world expedition must have been the source for several early European maps of the world. One of these is the 1507 map by Martin Waldseemüller, famous as the first map to feature the word "America." That map still exists and is owned by the Library of Congress.

Menzies contends that the Waldseemüller map shows San Francisco Bay, which wasn't "discovered" by European explorers until 1569—sixty-two years after the

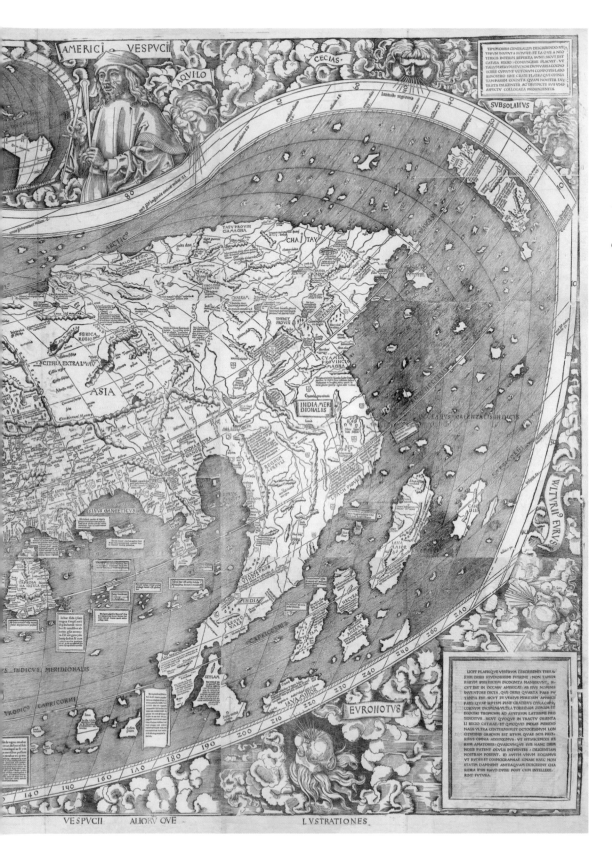

The famous Waldseemüller map of 1507. The continent of America appears at the far left.

map was published. Since no European had ever seen either San Francisco Bay or the west coast of North America when the Waldseemüller map appeared, the map must have been based on an earlier Chinese "master chart of the world," Menzies says. He believes that a copy of this chart was carried to Europe by Niccolò de Conti, a fifteenth-century Italian traveler who, according to Menzies, hitched a globe-trotting ride on one of Admiral Zheng's treasure ships. While no such "master chart" has yet been found, Menzies feels certain that one had to exist.

This interpretation of the Waldseemüller and several other early European maps doesn't satisfy many scholars. They point out that maps of that era were as much products of the imagination as they were accurate cartography. Early European mapmakers often included lands and seas inspired by legend rather than by actual exploration.

Menzies owns a large replica of the Waldseemüller map, so he was able to study it in detail. Only parts of Florida, a few Caribbean islands, and areas of Venezuela and Brazil are clearly visible on the map; European explorers had already charted those regions by 1507. On the western shores of North America, Waldseemüller drew some indistinct bluish mountains and wrote in bold type "Terra Ultra Incognita" (Land Beyond the Unknown). Yet Menzies is convinced that he can identify San Francisco Bay.

Moreover, he believes that the Chinese actually sailed into San Francisco Bay and sent at least one ship up the Sacramento River, where it ran aground and now rests beneath forty feet of river mud. As evidence for the

The Newport, Rhode Island, Tower. Did Chinese explorers build it?

wreck, he cites "a buried object 85 feet long and 30 feet wide, very similar in size and shape to the trading junks that accompanied Zheng He's treasure fleets." Menzies writes that some "strange armor" found at the site might have been of "medieval Chinese origin." However, the armor wasn't analyzed and has since been lost. And the "buried object" itself has never been positively identified.

As further evidence of global voyaging by the Chinese, Menzies cites a scattering of buried shipwrecks along the coasts of Oregon, California, Mexico, South America, and Florida that might conceal the remains of Chinese junks. Several big underwater sand mounds near the Bimini Islands in the Caribbean "may be the sand-covered hulls of treasure ships," he writes, "and they are just where I would expect to find the skeletons of junks swept ashore by a hurricane." So far, none of these mounds has been excavated. Scholars note that the Caribbean has been extensively explored by undersea archaeologists and treasure hunters, who are not likely to overlook such large wrecks. To date, no physical remains from any shipwreck have been conclusively identified as one of Zheng He's giant treasure ships.

Menzies's evidence seems shakiest when he cites the famous Newport Tower in Rhode Island and the mysterious Dighton Rock in Massachusetts. Over the years, people have claimed that the tower was built as an Indian lookout, a Viking outpost, a chapel for Irish monks, and a Portuguese watchtower. "It is more likely that the tower was erected by the Chinese" as a lighthouse and observatory, Menzies writes, because of its "striking resemblance" to a lighthouse built in southern China during the 1200s. While the tower's true origin is uncertain, most historians believe it was built as a windmill around 1650 by Rhode Island governor Benedict Arnold, great-great-grandfather of the Revolutionary War traitor.

Menzies also contends that the Chinese left carved stone markers at various places to record their voyages. One such stone, he argues, may be the ten-foot-high boulder known as the Dighton Rock in Massachusetts, thirty miles up the Taunton River from the Newport Tower. The boulder is covered with carved inscriptions that scholars have never been able to decipher. At one time or another, the inscriptions have been attributed to the ancient Scythians, Phoenicians, Vikings, Algonquin Indians, Portuguese explorers, and now, the Chinese.

Mysterious inscriptions on the Dighton Rock in Massachusetts.

After the Chinese built the Newport Tower, Menzies writes, they may have sailed up the Taunton River and inscribed the Dighton Rock as a marker to commemorate their journey. Over time the carved inscriptions have been worn away by river tides and winter ice and obscured by graffiti. "Whatever message the stone carried can no longer be read," Menzies laments. Eventually, the rock was moved to dry ground and installed in a small museum, where it can be seen, if not deciphered, today.

Historians have criticized Menzies's grab-bag approach to collecting evidence. "A chain is only as strong as its weakest link," says John E. Wills Jr. of the University of Southern California, and Menzies's links of evidence "are amazingly varied in quality."

Despite his unscholarly methods, Menzies is not necessarily wrong. Evidence of a Chinese influence in the Americas does in fact exist and has intrigued scholars for a long time. Professional historians should welcome the questions raised by an "obsessed amateur" such as Menzies, says Wills, because they focus public attention on issues that can give us all a clearer understanding of the past.

Following the seventh and last voyage of Zheng He's treasure fleets, in 1433, political upheavals in China led to an abrupt reversal of its foreign policy. The Chinese emperor banned overseas travel and halted all construction of oceangoing ships. The greatest navy the world had ever known was disbanded. Far from engaging the outside world, China turned inward, retreating into isolation. To prevent any renewal of the foreign expeditions, officials of the Chinese court burned many of Zheng He's sailing logs and records. If this hadn't happened, if China's age of exploration had continued, the world might be a very different place today. China rather than Europe might have conquered and colonized the New World of the Americas.

Because "almost every Chinese map and document of the period was deliberately destroyed," Menzies writes, hardly any evidence survived to show where the Chinese fleets sailed or what discoveries they made. Using the knowledge he had acquired during his years as a submarine commander on the high seas, Menzies set out to decipher the fragmentary evidence offered by ancient maps and charts, and by "those few documents and artifacts to have survived."

Menzies focuses on what he calls "the missing years" of Zheng's sixth voyage, between March 1421 and October 1423, when, he claims, the Chinese fleet sailed around the world. According to University of Arkansas historian Robert Finlay, a leading critic of Menzies, "There are plentiful surviving documents on the expeditions that prove there were no 'missing years.'" And there is no indication in those surviving records that the fleet sailed beyond Africa. "The voyages [Menzies] describes never took place," Finlay concludes.

A valuable source of information on Zheng He's voyages that still exists and has been translated into English is Ma Huan's *The Overall Survey of the Ocean's Shores*, first

Oceangoing junks like this fuchuan, *with its high prow and stern and wide, overhanging decks, may have provided a model for the bigger treasure ships. Considered one of the best pictures of a Chinese-style ship to be found in literature, this drawing from the* Liu-Chhiu Kuo Chih Lueh *of 1757 appears in* Science and Civilisation in China, *by Joseph Needham, 1954, vol. 4, pt. 3, figure 939, p. 405.*

printed in China in 1451. The author, an official translator on the staff of Admiral Zheng, sailed on three of Zheng's expeditions. His book is a survey of the places visited by Chinese fleets over several decades, rather than diaries of specific voyages, and he includes much information on countries he did not personally visit. Though Ma's account is a rich source of observations about foreign lands, he never mentions a voyage to the Americas.

Despite questions, doubts, and uncertainties, Menzies is confident that his theory will prove correct. An enthusiastic man with white hair, reddish eyebrows, and the tang of salt spray in his speech, he employs a staff of researchers who continue to check and evaluate new evidence that pours in from all over the world—reports of sunken Chinese junks, stories about Asian jade found in Aztec tombs, what appear to be Chinese ideograms found on pottery made in the Americas long before Columbus arrived. "The evidence grows by leaps and bounds every day," Menzies told a reporter.

An expedition of seagoing fuchuan, as depicted on an ancient Chinese scroll.

While many scholars are skeptical of Menzies's claims, they grant that some of the wrecks and artifacts he cites might be genuine Chinese remains, suggesting that small groups of Chinese seafarers actually did reach American shores from time to time. "Most scholars are generally agreed that there appears to have been at least some Asian influence in the New World before the arrival of Columbus," writes Louise Levathes, whose book *When China Ruled the Seas* is an authoritative history of the Chinese treasure fleets. "How much influence and exactly when this influence occurred are the subjects of much debate," she adds, "but one of the most likely moments of contact seems to be around 1000 B.C."—some 2,400 years before Zheng He.

At about that time, two widely separated civilizations in the Americas—the Chavin of the Peruvian Andes and the Olmec of Mexico's Gulf Coast—developed artistic traditions that were remarkably similar to certain arts being practiced by the Chinese. Chavin craftsmen fashioned stylized bronze figurines of jaguars that bear an astonishing resemblance to Chinese miniature statues of tigers from the same period. Like the Chinese tigers, the Peruvian jaguars have projecting teeth, and their bodies are covered with an intricate carved pattern. And they have distinctive rings on their tails that are found on living Asian tigers but not on South American jaguars.

In Mexico around the same time, Olmec artists began to fashion small, exquisitely carved jade sculptures and

The Kon Tiki Expedition. In 1947, Norwegian archaeologist Thor Heyerdahl and his six-man crew sailed 4,300 miles from South America to Polynesia aboard the balsawood and bamboo raft Kon Tiki, testing the theory that ancient cultures could have made such a journey on rafts driven by winds and ocean currents. Seafarers from ancient China may have used similar vessels to cross the Pacific in the opposite direction, landing in Central and South America.

figurines, including miniature human figures and personal ornaments such as beads and earrings. Like the Chinese, the Olmec used these jade objects as burial offerings in tombs. Was this a coincidence, or a sign of Asian influence in the New World?

According to Levathes, there are "strong indications" that as early as three thousand years ago, people from southeast Asia "successfully crossed the Pacific, landing in Central and South America." The boats that made this voyage are believed to be identical to the sailing rafts still used today by fishermen off the coasts of Taiwan, Vietnam, and Peru. Made of tightly bound balsa logs, they have a steering system that allows them to be maneuvered across the trade winds, and they can carry a hundred or more people in enclosed cabins. Spanish explorers arriving in South America during the 1500s reported seeing many of these sailing rafts, which were in constant use, ferrying goods and people up and down the coast faster, the Spaniards reported, than their own ships.

"The Chinese have been skilled and adventurous boatmen since the dawn of their civilization," Levathes writes. "Little doubt remains that there were Asian people in the New World before Columbus, and the evidence points to not one but several periods of contact."

Another period of contact may have occurred during the rise of the Mayan civilization in the fifth century A.D., when, according to Chinese records, Buddhist monks crossed the Pacific. The story, as recorded in the *Liang shu* (Official History of the Liang Dynasty), describes the voyage of Hui Shen and five fellow monks from present-day Afghanistan to a strange place called *Fusang quo*—"the Country of the Extreme East"—which some historians and archaeologists think was Central America, home of the Mayan civilization. Mayan art at that time suddenly began to include "a strong influx of Buddhist and Hindu elements," writes Levathes. Stone monuments from the Mayan city of Copan, for example, depict figures sitting cross-legged on lotus thrones, like meditating Buddhas, and priests wearing diamond-patterned ceremonial robes that look like traditional Buddhist robes. Scholars have also noted striking similarities between Chinese characters and square-shaped Mayan glyphs (a form of symbolic writing), and between the Chinese and Mayan calendars.

"Some outside Buddhist-Hindu influence on Mayan civilization seems likely," Levathes concludes, "whether it is attributable to Hui Shen and his Buddhist companions or to other Asian seafarers." So even if Zheng's treasure fleets never sailed past Africa, earlier Chinese seafarers may have made many landfalls in the Americas unrecorded in surviving documents—setting foot in places that Europeans would not see for centuries.

Like Columbus, those unsung Chinese explorers set out across uncharted seas, sailed to the world's edge and beyond, and discovered a new world. Then, it seems, they were nearly forgotten, leaving behind traces of their presence that continue to intrigue and challenge historians today.

This stone stela at the ancient Mayan city of Copan in present-day Honduras depicts a Mayan ruler wearing a diamond-patterned ceremonial robe similar to Buddhist robes.

Chapter Three

LEIF
THE LUCKY

I T WAS IN THE YEAR A.D. 1000, *or thereabouts, that Leif Eriksson, first son of Eric the Red, set out on his great adventure. With a sturdy ship and a crew of thirty-five hardy men, he sailed from Greenland in search of unexplored lands that had been sighted to the west.*

After being tossed about at sea for two days, they spotted land, cast anchor, put out a boat, and rowed ashore. The land they found was barren and desolate—no grass or trees, nothing but a vast flat slab of rock that stretched from the edge of the sea to towering glaciers covering highlands in the distance. This place seemed of little use. Leif then spoke to his companions: "I shall give this country a name and call it Helluland [stone-slab land]," he said.

They returned to their ship, put out to sea again, sailed south, and sighted a second land, where they went ashore. Here they found large forests sloping gently seaward and many beaches of white sand. "This place shall be named for

what it has to offer," said Leif. "I'll call it Markland [forest land]."

After this they hurried back to their ship and sailed to the southwest before they saw land again. Heading toward it, they came to an island, where they rowed ashore. The weather was fine. They found dew on the grass, which they collected in their hands and drank, and to them it seemed the sweetest thing they had ever tasted. Later they carried their sleeping sacks ashore, built shelters, and decided to spend the winter. Leif would name this place Vinland [wineland].

Leif Eriksson and his companions approach the coast of Vinland. An illustration by Oscar Arnold Wergeland, published in 1877.

Figurehead of the Viking ship Hugin—
a replica of a medieval Danish vessel.

The story of Leif Eriksson's voyage as it has come down to us is not an eyewitness account. It is a tale that was told and retold by generations of Scandinavians before it was finally written down as part of *The Vinland Sagas,* which tell of great men and women, of battles fought, heroic deeds, and new lands discovered during the height of the Viking Age. For some three hundred years, from the eighth to eleventh centuries, Viking explorers, traders, and warriors from Norway, Denmark, and Sweden, in search of land, slaves, and riches, raided all across Europe, established colonies, and voyaged as far as North Africa, Russia, and Constantinople.

By the time Leif's story was put into writing, more than two centuries had passed and the tale of his adventure had taken on a life of its own. Some details had faded from memory and been lost. Others had been embellished and ornamented in the imaginations of those who heard the sagas recited in Norse farmhouses beside roaring fires on long winter evenings.

Ever since the sagas were first translated into English in the early 1800s, they have been a subject of controversy and debate. Was Vinland a real place? If so, where was it located, and what actually happened there? Because no physical evidence of Vikings had been found in the New World (beyond Greenland), few historians took seriously the possibility that Viking explorers had reached the North American mainland five hundred years before Columbus. They regarded *The Vinland Sagas* as a collection of stories about what people remembered or thought they remembered of bygone times, an entertaining mixture of fact and fable. If Leif Eriksson and others really did explore North America, the sagas did not reveal the locations of any of the places they visited.

And yet the sagas could not be dismissed. They accurately identify certain historical facts, such as the dates of settlement of Iceland (during the last decades of the ninth century) and Greenland (around the year 985). Some of the descriptions in the sagas seem to match the northeast coast of North America.

Viking enthusiasts believed that Leif Eriksson not only landed in North America but ventured as far south as New England. It was said that Viking explorers were responsible for those mysterious rock carvings in Massachusetts that Gavin Menzies would later attribute to Chinese explorers. And the old stone tower in Newport, Rhode Island, that had puzzled historians for years was rumored to have been built not by Chinese but by a lovelorn Viking warrior.

Helge Ingstad, a Norwegian writer and explorer (and a self-taught historian, like Menzies), was convinced that *The Vinland Sagas* were based on fact and that Vikings had established a settlement in North America. Ingstad was regarded by many professional historians as one of those "obsessed amateurs" who claim to know better than the experts, and at first, his theory was dismissed.

For several years, Ingstad roamed coastal areas of New England, Nova Scotia, and Labrador, by foot, boat, and plane, traveling at his own expense and searching with-

Explorer Helge Ingstad points to the route he followed when he discovered a Viking settlement at L'Anse aux Meadows in Newfoundland, Canada.

out success for evidence of a Viking landfall. Finally, in the spring of 1960, following a hunch and an ancient map, he traveled to the fishing village of L'Anse aux Meadows (The Bay by the Meadows) at the northern tip of Newfoundland, a spot identified on an Icelandic map from the 1670s as "Promontorium Winlandiae."

Ingstad asked a local fisherman, George Decker, if there were any unusual ruins in the vicinity. "Yes," Decker told him. "Follow me."

"Decker took me west of the village to a beautiful place with lots of grass and a small creek and some mounds in the tall grass," Ingstad recalled. "It was very clear that this was a very, very old site. There were remains of sod walls. Fishermen assumed it was an old Indian site. But Indians didn't use that kind of buildings and houses."

Ingstad had studied Viking ruins in Greenland. And he suspected that these grass-covered mounds in Newfoundland concealed another Viking settlement. The following year he returned to the site with his wife, Anne Stine Ingstad, an archaeologist, and together they began the excavations that transformed a literary myth into scientific fact.

Archaeological digs by the Ingstads over several summers uncovered the foundations of houses, a bronze pin, a bone needle, a whetstone, and other objects dating from the tenth century that could have resulted only from a Norse occupation of the site. "The excavations were exciting from the moment we started digging, but often very difficult," Ingstad wrote. "True, conditions were not always so very pleasant—kneeling on the grass all day, come rain, wind, or fog, and scraping away inch after inch of soil is not the most comfortable way of life. But these discomforts were soon forgotten. And when we really came across a find, and careful work with the brush revealed something of Norse character—when that happened, it was like a miracle. Suddenly we felt that we almost knew those Norse people who had lived here so long ago."

For the first time, physical evidence proved conclusively that Norsemen, or Vikings, had landed in America five hundred years before Columbus. The Ingstads were convinced that they had found the camp occupied by Leif Eriksson and his companions, as described in *The Vinland Sagas*.

⚜

When Leif Eriksson was born, around A.D. 975, Viking raiders were still terrorizing much of Europe. Setting out in swift, sleek boats, they descended, sword in hand, upon coastal monasteries, towns, and villages, wherever they hoped to find rich booty. The speed and daring of their surprise attacks devastated seaside communities from the Irish Sea to the coasts of France and Spain.

By Leif's time, these lightning raids were beginning to taper off as Viking seafarers sought new lands for a growing population. They had been discovering and settling new territory in the North Atlantic since the early 800s. They may have learned of these lands from Irish monks, who in turn may have followed in the wake of Saint

Opposite: *Viking raiders approach the Normandy coast in this 1911 illustration by an unnamed artist.*

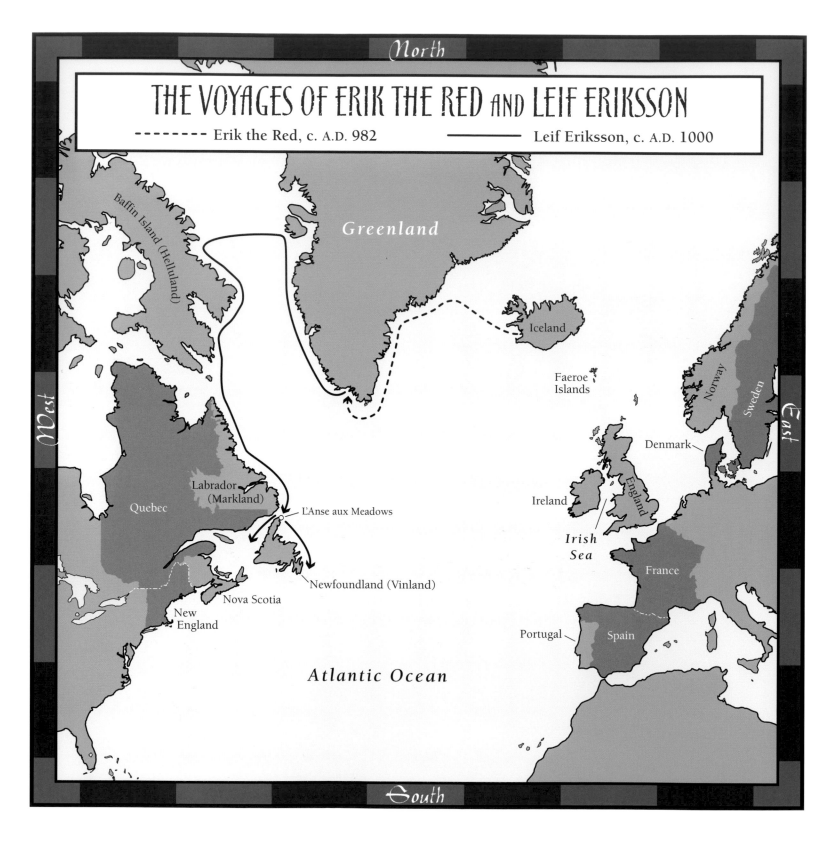

THE VOYAGES OF ERIK THE RED AND LEIF ERIKSSON

- - - - - - Erik the Red, c. A.D. 982   ——————— Leif Eriksson, c. A.D. 1000

North

West

East

South

Baffin Island (Helluland)

Greenland

Iceland

Faeroe Islands

Norway

Sweden

Denmark

Labrador (Markland)

Quebec

L'Anse aux Meadows

Ireland

England

Irish Sea

France

Newfoundland (Vinland)

Nova Scotia

New England

Portugal

Spain

Atlantic Ocean

Brendan, the sixth-century monk whose legendary voyage has inspired endless speculation.

Most of these seagoing pioneers came from farms on the long, jagged coast of Norway, where they struggled to make a meager living from small fields squeezed between rugged mountains and long fjords that cut deeply into the land. Looking to the sea for greater opportunities, they struck out from their sheltered fjords in sturdy Viking longships built to withstand fierce ocean storms.

Sailing without compasses or other instruments, without maps or charts, carried along by winds and swells, following the movements of birds, and navigating by the sun and the stars, they traveled from one island to the next in little more than a two- or three-day sail. Viking settlers had reached the Faeroe Islands, some 350 miles west of Norway, by the year 825. They colonized Iceland, 600 miles west of Norway, starting in 870. By 930, Iceland was already overcrowded with a population of 30,000, and all of its best farmland had been taken.

Leif Eriksson's father, known as Erik the Red for his shock of thick red hair and his fiery temper, was an immigrant from Norway who farmed a small plot of land in Iceland and had a reputation as an unpredictable hothead. In 982, when Leif was a child, Erik was accused of killing two men during an argument and was banished from Iceland for three years. He spent his years of exile exploring the coastline of an unknown land several days' sail to the west that had been sighted by voyagers blown off course on their way to Iceland.

Erik called this far northern land Greenland because of

the lush meadows he found in sheltered valleys along the land's fjords. He also may have figured that an appealing name like "Greenland" would help attract settlers. *The Vinland Sagas* tell how Erik returned to Iceland, organized a group of colonists, and set out for Greenland with twenty-five heavily loaded ships. While the climate in the North Atlantic was warmer then than it is today, the seas between Iceland and Greenland were often stormy and ice filled, and the crossing was perilous. Only fourteen of the twenty-five ships in Erik's fleet reached their destination safely.

Erik claimed a choice location for his own farm, where

Erik the Red, his ship surrounded by icebergs and whales, discovers the coast of Greenland. An 1875 illustration from Harper's Weekly.

he raised a big family and earned respect as leader of the island's growing Norse community. Meanwhile, stories were circulating about heavily wooded lands that had been sighted even farther to the west by sailors driven off course during a storm. Greenland's coasts were grassy but treeless. Excited by the prospect of exploring new territory and perhaps finding better opportunities than Greenland offered, Erik and his three sons talked of going to sea again.

According to the sagas, Erik planned to lead the expedition, but as he was riding down to join his ship, his horse stumbled. Fearing that this was a bad omen, a sure

Leif Eriksson points to shore as he steers his ship through heavy seas. This engraving, from a painting by Norwegian artist Christian Krohg, was published in 1911.

sign of trouble ahead, he decided to stay home. His eldest son, Leif, known as Leif the Lucky, took his father's place and became the first to head for these unexplored lands beyond the western horizon.

The sagas describe Leif as "tall and strong and very impressive in appearance. He was a shrewd man and always moderate in his behavior." Growing up in Greenland, where skilled seamanship was a necessity, he became an able mariner before he was out of his teens. Later, he earned his nickname after rescuing fifteen shipwrecked men on the high seas and being rewarded with a box of gold and silver jewelry.

With his crew of thirty-five men, Leif set out from Greenland and sailed toward the setting sun. Carried along by the Labrador Current, accompanied by massive floating icebergs, by flocks of Atlantic puffins and flightless great auks, they sailed along the barren, rocky coastlines of Baffin Island (which he named Helluland) and continued south along the forested coast of Labrador (Markland) until they reached the northern tip of Newfoundland (Vinland). It was here that Leif Eriksson and his companions established the first European settlement in North America—the site visited by Helge Ingstad and his archaeologist wife in 1961.

❧

The silent ruins at L'Anse aux Meadows provide a window into the past. They tell the story of the people who settled there briefly, when they arrived, and what they did.

Below: *One of the reconstructed Viking longhouses at L'Anse aux Meadows National Historic Site in Newfoundland, Canada. Visitors can explore its six rooms, which include three main dwelling rooms with their central hearths, a combination kitchen-sauna, a storage room, and a work shed.*

Right: *A reconstruction of the Vikings' smithy, or blacksmith shop, where the first iron was forged in the New World.*

Archaeologists estimate the age of ruins by the type of architecture; by artifacts found in the immediate area, such as tools, weapons, and ornaments; and by radio-carbon dating—measuring the amount of carbon 14 found in organic objects such as bones, wood, cloth, and plant fibers. Because carbon 14 disintegrates at a known rate over time after a person, animal, or plant dies, it can be used to determine the approximate age of ancient archaeological specimens.

The Viking ruins at L'Anse aux Meadows occupy a spectacular setting on a wide grassy cove overlooking Epaves Bay and the Strait of Belle Isle beyond. Archaeologists have found the foundations of eight buildings dating back to around A.D. 1000. The design of the longhouses and other buildings is similar to that of structures built in Iceland around that time. The solid construction—thick sod walls and roofs over wooden frames—indicates that

they were built for year-round use. And the size of the living areas—with their huge fireplaces and combination kitchen-saunas—suggests that some ninety people could have lived in the settlement. Smaller buildings on the site included a carpentry shop, identified by hundreds of wood chips and shavings, which was probably used for ship repairs, and a smithy, where iron was forged, most likely to make new boat nails. Dozens of snipped and discarded nails were found at the site. A smithy had to have been Norse made—no such technology existed among the native inhabitants.

Among the artifacts uncovered at L'Anse aux Meadows were a stone lamp, an ornamental bronze pin, a bone needle, a soapstone spindle whorl (part of a thread-spinning kit), and a small whetstone of the kind used by Norse women to sharpen needles, scissors, and knives. Since weaving and sewing were considered women's work, these finds show that women were present at the site.

The settlement was the year-round base camp from which the Vikings explored a wide area. The discovery of two butternuts, or white walnuts, along with wood from a butternut tree, reveals a great deal about the Vikings' travels. Early on, there were objections to identifying L'Anse aux Meadows as the Vinland site, because grapes don't grow that far north. Neither do butternuts. To find butternut trees, the settlers would have had to make excursions to warmer areas farther south—perhaps to the Saint Lawrence River valley near present-day Quebec City. Since wild grapes grow in the same areas as butternut trees, the person who picked the nuts must have

Among the artifacts found at L'Anse aux Meadows was this soapstone spindle whorl, once part of a thread-spinning kit.

The discovery of this butternut revealed a great deal about the Vikings' travels.

ANNE STINE OG HELGE INGSTAD

De oppdaget vikingenes Amerika

This statue of archaeologist Anne Stine Ingstad and her husband, explorer Helge Ingstad, greets visitors at the entrance to the L'Anse aux Meadows Historic Site.

found grapevines as well. And so *The Vinland Sagas'* tales about finding wild grapes in the region are fact rather than fancy. This explains why Leif gave the name Vinland (wineland) to the area explored by the Vikings. Butternuts and grapes were brought back to the Viking camp at L'Anse aux Meadows, where they were stored over the winter to be taken back to Greenland.

Leif and his crew spent one winter at the Viking camp. "In the spring," the sagas tell us, "they made ready to leave and sailed away. . . . They put out to sea and had favorable winds all the way until they sighted Greenland and its ice-capped mountains." They were carrying a full cargo of timber and towing behind their ship a boat "filled with grapes."

Leif may have intended to return to Vinland himself, but when his father, Erik, died, Leif took over for him as leader of the Norse community and remained in Greenland. However, members of Leif's family made several more voyages to Vinland, occupying their base at L'Anse aux Meadows for perhaps ten years and exploring regions to the north and south. They gathered valuable resources not available in Greenland, including hardwoods for shipbuilding and grapes for wine.

The settlement was made up of sailors, carpenters, blacksmiths, hired hands, and perhaps even serfs or slaves captured during Viking raids in Europe. Some of the men brought their wives. The last few expeditions to Vinland were led by Thorfinn Karlsefni, an Icelandic trader who was married to Leif's widowed sister-in-law, Gudrid. It was at L'Anse aux Meadows that the first

European child in the Americas was born, a boy named Snorri, the son of Gudrid and Thorfinn.

The sagas hint at what little is known about contacts between the Vikings and the native Americans they encountered. We can only imagine how the two groups reacted when first they met. To the Indians, the oddly dressed strangers who appeared so unexpectedly in their midst must have seemed very strange. They wore heavy, brightly colored garments and had blue eyes, pale skin, and blond or reddish hair. And they carried iron swords and axes glittering with copper and silver decorations— axes that were sharp enough to cut off a man's head with a single blow.

To the Vikings, the dark-haired people they encountered as they explored the forests of Vinland and Markland may have seemed similar to the native people who still lived in the northern regions of Greenland. They called both groups *skraelings,* a disparaging Norse term. And yet the Norse were a long way from their home base in Greenland now. They had ventured deeply into alien territory, into unfamiliar forests where their small exploratory parties were greatly outnumbered by the native inhabitants. So both Vikings and Indians must have been apprehensive as well as curious as they stood cautiously eyeing each other.

According to the sagas, brief attempts at trade were followed by misunderstandings and outbreaks of violence. After the Vikings killed eight *skraelings* who were sleeping under skin canoes, Leif's brother Thorvald was killed by an Indian arrow. Today it is impossible to know exactly what happened, since the saga accounts were not written down until at least two centuries after the events they describe.

Thorfinn Karlsefni had hoped to establish a permanent colony in Vinland, but clashes with the Indians discouraged him. The Vikings, who numbered no more than ninety or a hundred, felt that they would never be safe in Vinland because of the many native inhabitants, and after a few years they gave up their base at L'Anse aux Meadows and returned to Greenland. Vinland was "a rich and fruitful land," said Thorfinn, "but one which we cannot safely inhabit."

Leif's brother Thorvald lies mortally wounded during a battle between Viking settlers and local Indians in this undated illustration by an artist named Kendrick, otherwise not identified.

The American Viking boat Snorri, *built in Maine, heads past an island near L'Anse aux Meadows in July 2000. The replica vessel was part of a flotilla that visited the historic site, honoring Leif Eriksson's voyage a thousand years earlier.*

Although the Vinland explorations ended, Norse seafarers continued to visit North America during the next four centuries to obtain lumber for treeless Greenland and to trade with the native peoples. Norse artifacts—including iron tools, woolen cloth, a carpenter's wood plane, and even a fragment of a bronze scale—have been found at several Native American archaeological sites in the Canadian Arctic. These trading voyages continued until the early 1400s, when the Norse colonies in Greenland were abandoned as the climate turned colder and the population outstripped the island's limited resources.

Did Christopher Columbus know about the Viking visits to North America? Some scholars believe that he may have learned about them from *The Vinland Sagas* when he visited Iceland with the crew of a Portuguese ship in 1477. Even so, when Columbus reached San Salvador, he thought he was near India—not in the far north.

Chapter Four

THE NOT-SO-NEW WORLD

COLUMBUS AND THE EUROPEAN explorers who followed him looked upon the Americas as a promising New World. It may have been a "new" and unknown world to them, but to the tens of millions of people already living there, the Native Americans, it was home and had been for untold thousands of years.

By some estimates, more people were living in the Americas when Columbus sailed than lived in all of Europe. The central Mexican plateau, heartland of the Aztec empire, may have contained as many as 25 million people, compared to fewer than 10 million living in Spain and Portugal. That would have made Mexico the most densely populated place on Earth at the time, with more people per square mile than China or India.

Early explorers were amazed at the throngs of people they encountered. In 1542, Father Bartolomé de Las Casas, a Spanish missionary, described the New World as

a crowded, bustling place, "a bee hive of people," a land so populous "that it looked as if God has placed all of or a greater part of the entire human race in these countries." At about the same time, Hernando de Soto, traveling with his army through the Mississippi valley, described a countryside "thickly set with great towns . . . two or three [towns] to be seen from one."

Across the Americas, native peoples spoke some 1,200 separate languages. Some lived in cities larger than any in Europe. They had invented more than a dozen different systems of writing, devised calendars as accurate as any in use today, and built astronomical observatories from which they tracked the orbits of the planets. And they

A pair of tourists explores the Mayan ruins of Tikal in Guatemala. The largest ancient city of the Mayan civilization, Tikal flourished more than a thousand years ago before its mysterious decline in the ninth century A.D.

belonged to almost every imaginable kind of human society, from small roving bands of hunters and gatherers to immensely rich and powerful empires that ruled millions of people.

Complex civilizations had existed long before the Europeans arrived. Often they were built on foundations laid by much older cultures. By 1492, native peoples had inhabited the Americas for more generations than anyone could count. Their ancestors had come from different places at different times in waves of migration, spreading slowly through the vast expanse of two continents, colonizing this New World they had "discovered," settling down where conditions were most favorable.

These diverse Native Americans, who varied in language, customs, and appearance as much as the different nationalities of Europe did, became known to the Europeans simply as "Indians." They didn't call themselves Indians, of course. "Indian" was Columbus's term. Rather, they identified themselves by the names of their particular tribes or communities.

The familiar war-bonneted Indian of the Wild West, chasing buffalo on horseback across the North American plains, didn't exist in 1492. Wild horses did once roam the grasslands of the Americas, but they disappeared thousands of years before Columbus and his followers introduced the first modern horses to the New World. Until then, native peoples hunted buffalo and other game on foot. And they did not necessarily depend on big-game hunting. Throughout the Americas, most Indians lived on farms.

Hunting on foot before the acquisition of horses, Natchez Indians close in on a small herd of buffalo. An eighteenth-century drawing by the French chronicler Antoine Simon Le Page du Pratz.

North America wasn't the untamed wilderness that many people imagine. Along the tree-lined rivers of the Great Plains, well-ordered Mandan and Hidatsa villages were surrounded by flourishing fields of maize, or Indian corn. In the arid southwest, the Hopis raised twenty-four varieties of corn and other crops on irrigated terraces below each village. On the Atlantic seaboard, the forests had been cut back from the coasts, which were lined with fields of corn, squash, and beans that in many places extended for miles into the interior. As a rule, women tended the crops, while men engaged in hunting and fishing.

A Wichita village of thatched-roof houses clustered at the center of radiating cornfields. The artist was an army captain who traveled through Wichita country in what is now eastern Oklahoma in the early nineteenth century.

To the south, in Mexico, Peru, and elsewhere, native peoples cultivated an enormous number of different plants. Corn, potatoes, cacao, pumpkins, peanuts, avocados, tomatoes, and pineapples, all grown by Native Americans, were unknown to Europeans and the rest of the world in 1492.

On the east coast of North America, European explorers and settlers were fascinated by the Indians' democratic traditions and by their insistence on personal liberty and social equality. People in Indian villages were not divided into upper and lower classes, as they were in Europe. Every member of a village was considered equal to everyone else; no one had the right to deprive others of their freedom. The Iroquois held "such absolute notions of liberty that they allow of no kind of superiority of one over another, and banish all servitude from their territories," declared Cadwallader Colden, a political leader in colonial New York and an adopted member of the Mohawk nation.

The Mohawks belonged to an alliance of five (later six) nations bound together by a common Iroquois language. They were known to themselves as the Haudenosaunee (People of the Longhouse), and to American colonists of the 1700s as the Iroquois Confederacy. Each member nation governed itself, but they acted together in time of war and met to confer on issues that concerned them all. This military and political alliance made the Iroquois the most powerful Indians in eastern America.

"At the Iroquois council fire": a 1901 magazine illustration.

The Confederacy was governed by a constitution, the Great Law of Peace, kept in memory and passed through oral tradition from one generation to the next. According to the Great Law, leaders of the allied nations, meeting as the Great Council, had to submit important matters to a decision of all their people. Decisions were reached through a process of consensus—in a kind of referendum open to both men and women.

Benjamin Franklin and other colonial leaders attended treaty negotiations with members of the Indian nations' Great Council and were impressed by the way the allied tribes acted together. If the Iroquois could establish a

North

North
America

Mandans
& Hidatsas

Iroquois
(Haudenosaunees)

Pacific Ocean

Atlantic Ocean

Hopis

Mexico

Olmecs

Tenochtitlán
(Mexico City)

Mayas

Aztecs

Caribbean Sea

Central
America

Incas

Peru

South
America

Aspero

Caral

Norte Chico

Lima

Andes Mountains

Cuzco

West

East

NATIVE AMERICA,
c. 2700 B.C.–A.D. 1492

Advanced civilizations had been
rising and falling for thousands of
years before Europeans arrived.
The societies shown here did not all
exist at the same time—the Olmecs
vanished centuries before the Aztecs
began to reach their height, for
example. This map indicates the
heartland of each society.

South

powerful union, Franklin wondered, then why couldn't a union be formed by the thirteen American colonies, "to whom it is more necessary, and must be more advantageous"? Some historians have argued that the Great Law of Peace directly inspired the United States Constitution.

&

Many of the native tribes and nations in North America shared the democratic spirit of the Iroquois. But customs were very different in Mexico and South America, where two large and powerful civilizations were at the peak of their influence. The Aztec empire had conquered most of central and southern Mexico, sent out colonies, and spread vast networks of trade. The emperor, Montezuma II, was regarded as a godlike figure. Important chiefs who accompanied Montezuma walked ahead of him, sweeping the path where he would pass, putting down mats so he would not have to step on the ground. "None of these lords thought of looking in his face," reported a Spanish eyewitness. "All of them kept their eyes down, with great reverence."

Montezuma ruled over a society that was sharply divided between nobles who lived in luxury and the great mass of commoners, indentured workers, and slaves. Most slaves had been captured in battle; they were bought and sold at markets like any other commodity. Many ended their lives as human sacrifices to the Aztec Sun God.

The Aztec capital, Tenochtitlán, a glittering metropolis of artificial islands and canals in the middle of a great

The Spanish conquistador Hernando Cortés kneels before Montezuma II, the Aztec emperor, in this 1878 illustration from Frank Leslie's Popular Monthly.

The great temple and plaza of Tenochtitlán, the Aztec capital at the site occupied today by Mexico City. A sixteenth-century reconstruction by Ignacio Marguina.

mountain lake, had more people than Paris or London. Three giant causeways linked the island city to the mainland. Long aqueducts carried fresh water from distant mountains across Lake Texcoco and into heart of the city. And a workforce of a thousand men swept the wide, tree-lined city streets and kept them immaculately clean.

Spanish invaders led by Hernando Cortés were dazzled by the wealth and beauty of Tenochtitlán. They gaped at ornately carved and painted palaces, at magnificent temples perched atop tall pyramids, and at the city's zoological and botanical gardens—nothing of the sort existed in Europe. "We were astounded," one of Cortés's men reported. "The pyramids and buildings rising from the water, all made of stone, seemed like an enchanted vision. . . . Indeed, some of our soldiers asked whether it was not all a dream."

The arrival of Cortés and his tough little army, with their fire-spitting weapons, snarling dogs, and frightening horses, proved a disaster for the Aztecs. The Spaniards were joined by thousands of Indian allies—warriors from tribes that had been conquered and brutally exploited by the Aztecs—and the combined forces attacked the imperial capital in 1520–21.

After a siege lasting more than fifteen weeks, Tenochtitlán fell into Spanish hands. By then, the great city lay in ruins. Three quarters of the population had been killed during the fighting or had died of starvation or from the ravages of smallpox, bringing an end to the mighty Aztec empire. "Our heritage became a net made of holes," lamented an Aztec sage, "when our cries of grief rose up and our tears rained down."

An even larger empire had come to power in South America. In less than a hundred years, the Incas had transformed themselves from a small, insignificant tribe into the conquering rulers of a vast domain that stretched three thousand miles from the rainforests of the Amazon across the snowcapped peaks of the Andes to the deserts of the Peruvian coast. Linking the far-flung provinces was the world's most extensive road system, the royal road of the Incas—a marvelously engineered network of stone-paved thoroughfares that cut through granite mountain slopes and converged on the sacred city of Cuzco in the Andean highlands of Peru.

The ruins of Machu Picchu, the great fortress city of the Incas, perched high in the southern Andes between two sharp mountain peaks.

Francisco Pizarro and his army of Spanish conquistadors gasped in disbelief when they first laid eyes on the splendors of Cuzco. The ceremonial plaza at the heart of the city, the length of two modern football fields, was carpeted with pure white sand brought in from the Pacific and raked daily by an army of workers. Lining the plaza on three sides stood magnificent palaces and temples, their granite walls clad with enormous sheets of polished gold.

An Inca official holds a quipu, a series of knotted strings of varying colors used for accounting and calculation. Drawing by Felipe Guamán Poma de Ayala, the native Peruvian chronicler of Inca life.

Beyond the imperial capital lay other monumental cities, temples and fortresses of stone, massive irrigated farming terraces, suspension bridges across mountain ravines, highways, and canals. To help keep track of this sprawling empire, the Incas used a unique form of record keeping—sequences of knots on strings called *quipus* that formed a binary code not unlike that of today's computer languages.

The Incan empire was the largest ever forged in the Americas—and the shortest lived, lasting only about a century. By the time Pizarro and his small band of conquistadors arrived on the scene in 1530, the empire was already near collapse, weakened by a raging plague of smallpox. The alien disease brought by Europeans had swept down from Mexico and was now ravaging the peoples of the central Andes. Meanwhile, unrest among recently conquered tribes and bitter rivalries between ruling families had erupted into open rebellion and civil war.

Pizarro played the warring factions against each other. With only about 180 men, 62 horses, and one cannon, he was able to smash Incan resistance. The death of the last

Incan emperor, killed on Pizarro's orders, marked the beginning of a long period of Spanish domination.

⚡

Advanced civilizations had been rising and falling in the Americas for thousands of years before Europeans arrived. In Mexico and parts of Central America, the Mayas built dozens of kingdoms and independent city-states that flourished for several hundred years before falling victim to a long-term decline. By A.D. 900, the greatest Mayan cities, with their spectacular palaces, temples, and pyramids, had been emptied and the countryside around them abandoned—a collapse that is still not fully understood. Among Mayan accomplishments were a sophisticated written language and mathematical system, extremely precise calendars, and the introduction of chocolate to a grateful world. Chocolate was consumed as a frothy drink made of ground cocoa beans flavored with spices and sweetened with honey. Cocoa beans were valued so highly, they were used as a form of currency.

Before the Mayas, a mysterious people called the Olmecs appeared in Mexico around 1500 B.C. They too built carefully planned cities, great earthwork pyramids topped by temples, and massive stone monuments. Digging around the ruins of their temples, archaeologists have unearthed colossal heads of stone, many six feet tall or more, with helmetlike headgear and amazingly realistic facial expressions. The apparent African features of these sculpted heads has led some scholars to speculate that the Olmecs either were visited by Africans or actu-

Archaeologists examine an ancient Mayan monument in the jungles of Guatemala. Photographed between 1890 and 1925.

ally migrated from Africa. According to these scholars, Africans may have "discovered" America before the Europeans.

Moving even further back in history, archaeologists have uncovered the remains of an almost 5,000-year-old pyramided city called Caral in the Norte Chico region of Peru, about 120 miles north of Lima. Caral's pyramids date back to around 2700 B.C.—when the first great pyramids in Egypt were being built. The city, with its elaborate complex of temples, ceremonial plazas, an amphitheater, and residential apartment buildings, spread over

This stone sculpture of a human head was found among Olmec ruins near San Lorenzo, Mexico. It is nine feet tall, six feet wide, and twenty feet around.

some 150 acres. Among the artifacts uncovered at the site are musical instruments—flutes made of pelican bones and horns of deer and llama bones. Also found was a *quipu,* the knotted-string writing system still being used by the Incas four millennia later.

Other ancient urban centers in the Norte Chico region may be as much as a thousand years older than Caral, and one, Aspero, which has not been fully excavated, might turn out to be the oldest known city of the New World.

Before the earliest cities were built, there were small settlements where native peoples farmed and temporary campsites visited by roving bands of hunters and gatherers. Many of those prehistoric residents of the Americas vanished without a trace, but others left unmistakable evidence of their presence—human footprints, the charred remains of ancient cooking fires, and stone spearheads made with care by human hands in an age when a stone weapon could mean mastery over nature as well as the difference between life and death.

A panoramic view of the ruins of Caral, one of the oldest known cities in the Americas.

Chapter Five

WHO REALLY DISCOVERED AMERICA?

A tooth from a prehistoric woolly mammoth, found buried in Ohio.

FIRST THEY FOUND A SKELETON: the ancient bones of a giant woolly mammoth buried in a dried-up lake bed near Clovis, New Mexico.

Then, as archaeologists uncovered the mammoth's bones, they spotted a lethal Stone Age weapon. Lying next to the skeleton was a large stone spearhead. Evidently, the mammoth had been killed by hunters hurling a spear with the sharp stone point attached to its tip.

The Clovis spearhead was discovered in 1933. Later, archaeologists were able to carbon-date the mammoth's bones and estimate the age of the spearhead. It was roughly 13,500 years old—the oldest human artifact found in the Americas up to that time. The discovery proved that humans were living in North America alongside mammoths, giant sloths, saber-toothed tigers, and other Ice Age creatures that are now extinct.

Diorama of prehistoric hunters spearing a mammoth.

Since then, thousands of Clovis spearheads have been found at archaeological sites all over North America and as far south as Costa Rica. The people who made these Stone Age weapons chiseled rough pieces of rock into four-inch-long pointed projectiles, skillfully flaked on both sides, with sharp serrated edges resembling the teeth of a saw. This design, archaeologists believe, allowed hunters to rapidly load and reload the spearheads onto the tips of wooden shafts. Hurled at an animal, the sharply pointed blade would remain embedded in the animal's flesh as the hunter pulled out the shaft, quickly backed away, loaded a new stone point, and was ready to hunt again.

Experiments with replicas of Clovis spearheads have shown that those deadly projectiles were effective against even the biggest animals. Archaeologists found that the spearheads could penetrate the tough hide of circus elephants that had died of natural causes.

Along with spearheads used for hunting, Clovis people left behind at their prehistoric campsites stone tools for gathering plants and for working wood, bone, and animal hides. Archaeologists have found punches or awls designed to help sew leather clothing. A 13,000-year-old stone blade the size of a dinner knife was apparently used to cut grass, which could have been used to make baskets, bedding, and thatched roofs for shelter.

Because Clovis sites were the oldest ever found in the Americas, archaeologists figured that Clovis people were the earliest Americans. But where had they come from? When did they arrive? And how did they travel to what truly was a New World?

The Earth's climate some 13,000 years ago provides a clue. Clovis hunters were making tools in North America when the last great Ice Age was nearing its end. At that time, much of the Northern Hemisphere lay frozen under gigantic sheets of polar ice. Because the ice locked up enormous amounts of water, sea levels around the world were hundreds of feet lower than they are today, exposing a wide strip of dry land that connected Siberia and Alaska. Today, this Ice Age land bridge, known as Beringia, lies submerged beneath the waters of the Bering Strait.

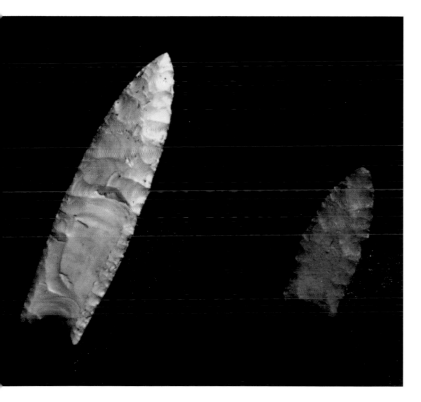

Clovis spear points. The larger spear point is five inches long.

Fur-clad hunters in pursuit of big game could have crossed the fifty-three-mile land bridge easily, actually hiking from Siberia to Alaska. From there, they might have made their way south through an ice-free corridor that opened toward the end of the Ice Age as the climate warmed and the glaciers began to recede. Bounded on either side by towering walls of retreating glaciers, this narrow, treeless ice-free corridor cut through the center of present-day Canada, reaching all the way south to the Great Plains, which were covered with grass and teeming with game.

Geologists calculated that the Bering land bridge and the ice-free corridor existed around the same time that Clovis tool makers first appeared in North America. This led to the "Clovis First" theory—the idea that around

Archaeologist Lee Bement removes dirt from a buried bison bone at a site in Oklahoma where Clovis spearheads were found.

13,500 years ago these people walked across the land bridge from Siberia to Alaska, trekked south through the ice-free corridor, and became America's first immigrants.

The story of this epic journey was so convincing, it was widely accepted for more than half a century and can still be found in many textbooks. But during the 1980s, as new evidence came to light, the Clovis First theory was brought into question. Recent discoveries suggest that it was almost certainly wrong.

The most startling new evidence comes from Monte Verde, an archaeological site in southern Chile, near the tip of South America. There, about 14,500 years ago, a band of hunters and gatherers lived beside a creek in a long oval animal-hide tent, partitioned with logs. Archaeologists spent the 1980s and 1990s unearthing the remains of this ancient encampment. Along with the remains of stone tools and the hide tent, preserved under a layer of waterlogged peat, they found two pieces of uneaten mastodon meat, traces of plants still used today in South America as herbal medicines, and three human footprints.

If people were living at Monte Verde 14,500 years ago, a thousand years before the earliest known Clovis people, they must have crossed over from Asia much earlier than that in order to make their way on foot from the Bering Strait to the tip of South America—a distance of some 10,000 miles. They couldn't have passed down the ice-free corridor, because it didn't exist yet. In fact, the latest studies indicate that the ice sheets were bigger and longer lasting than had previously been thought, and that the ice-free corridor didn't open until around 12,000 years ago—too late to have served as a route even for the Clovis people. While Ice Age hunters could have gone on foot across the Bering land bridge from Siberia to Alaska, giant ice sheets would have blocked their entrance to the rest of the continent. Without the ice-free corridor, it is hard to imagine how the Clovis people, the Monte Verde people, or anyone else could have traveled overland from Alaska to the south.

The mystery deepened as new prehistoric sites were discovered in both North and South America that appear to be even older than Monte Verde. At a place called Meadowcroft near Pittsburgh, Pennsylvania, archaeologists digging since the 1970s have uncovered apparent tools and the remains of ancient fire pits dating back some 18,000 years. Sites in Virginia and South Carolina may be as old or considerably older.

While archaeologists dig into the past, searching for the remains of prehistoric campsites, other researchers have been studying DNA to learn about patterns of human migrations. DNA is a chemical messenger that transmits hereditary information (such as eye color and nose shape) from one generation to the next. By analyzing slight changes in DNA that take place over time, geneticists can trace human ancestry far back into the past. Their research suggests that there were probably several different waves of migration to the Americas, and that the earliest migrants arrived from Siberia and northeast Asia between 20,000 and 30,000 years ago. Researchers who specialize in linguistics, the study of languages and how they develop, have come to a similar conclusion.

Left: *In the waters off Neah Bay, Washington, on December 16, 1998, a Makah whaler practices by harpooning a float in preparation for the Makah Indians' first whale hunt in 78 years. So much time had passed since the last Makah hunt in 1920, there was no one still alive who knew how to hunt a whale, as their ancestors had done for thousands of years.*

Right: *Ice Age immigrants from Siberia may well have reached North America by a sea route—probably in boats much larger than this one, manned by Inuit whalers in the Canadian Arctic.*

If the earliest Americans didn't travel down an ice-free corridor, then how did they get here? Many researchers now believe that prehistoric migrants from Asia may have followed a sea route along the Pacific coast, perhaps in skin-covered boats similar to those used today by the Inuit, native peoples of the Arctic. Hunting for seals, walruses, and other sea mammals, steering clear of glaciers and icebergs, early immigrants could have paddled along the southern edge of the Bering land bridge, then voyaged down the coast of Alaska, gradually advancing farther and farther south as each new generation staked out fresh hunting grounds a few miles beyond the last. Eventually, they reached the beaches of Central and South America, and finally, over many centuries, they arrived at Monte Verde. Meanwhile, their ancestors along the Pacific Coast had started to move inland, in the north becoming, perhaps, the Clovis people. Stone tools and the remains of human skeletons dating back 13,000 years have been found on islands off Alaska, California, and

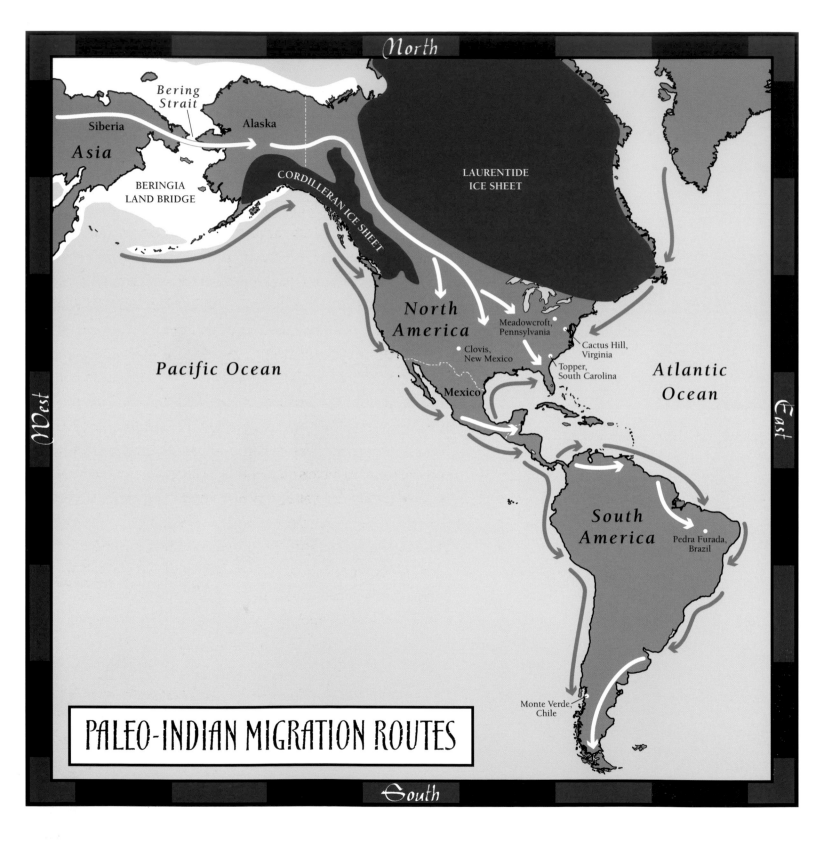

North

Bering
Strait

Siberia   Alaska

Asia

BERINGIA
LAND BRIDGE

CORDILLERAN ICE SHEET

LAURENTIDE
ICE SHEET

North
America

Meadowcroft,
Pennsylvania

Clovis,
New Mexico

Cactus Hill,
Virginia

Topper,
South Carolina

Pacific Ocean

Mexico

Atlantic
Ocean

West

East

South
America

Pedra Furada,
Brazil

Monte Verde,
Chile

PALEO-INDIAN MIGRATION ROUTES

South

Mexico, suggesting that people may have been traveling the coastal route by boat at least that early.

A few archaeologists have suggested another possibility—that Stone Age seafarers sailed to America from Europe, skirting the southern fringes of the great ice sheets that covered the North Atlantic and arriving on the eastern seaboard. This theory was prompted by the unexpected discovery that Clovis spearheads, found across North America, are not like the spearheads made by Ice Age hunters in Siberia. Instead, the Clovis projectiles closely resemble spearheads made in Europe by people known as the Solutreans, who lived in Ice Age Spain and France. Clovis and Solutrean spearheads not only look alike, they were also made in much the same way.

DNA studies suggest that the earliest Americans came from Asia, yet the Clovis spearhead is nowhere to be found in Asia. If Clovis people did, in fact, migrate from Siberia, why were they carrying spears that resembled Ice Age European spears? Could the Clovis spearhead and at least some of the earliest Americans actually have come from Europe? And if the Solutreans really did carry their spearheads across the icy Atlantic with them, then why have no other traces of their rich and varied culture been found in the Americas? They were the people who created some of Europe's great prehistoric cave paintings, as well as intricate carvings in bone, antler, and ivory.

Archaeologists have found no evidence that the Solutreans built boats capable of crossing the icy waters of the North Atlantic—or for that matter, any boats at all. Perhaps such evidence is missing, submerged under hundreds of feet of water as rising sea levels flooded the Solutrean coastline at the end of the Ice Age.

If the Solutreans really did journey to America, shouldn't DNA evidence reveal clues to their presence? DNA samples from a Native American tribe called the Ojibwa, from the Great Lakes region, suggest a link with certain European populations going back at least 15,000 years. And yet it's possible that this ancient genetic lineage may have once existed in Siberia as well and died out, but not before coming over to America with early migrations. So the DNA evidence doesn't give us an answer. It could be either from Europe or from a Siberian population that is now lost.

Could the similarities between Clovis and Solutrean spearheads be coincidental? "These were people faced with similar problems," says Lawrence Straus, a Solutrean expert at the University of New Mexico. "And the problems involved hunting large and medium-sized game with a similar, limited range of raw materials. . . . They're going to come up with similar solutions."

And while the Clovis and Solutrean spearheads resemble each other closely, they're not identical. "The actual point itself is unique to the Americas, suggesting that it was invented here in the New World," says Ken Tankersley of Northern Kentucky University. That would make the Clovis spearhead the first great American invention.

Amidst all the competing theories and spirited scientific debates, it seems clear that the Clovis people were

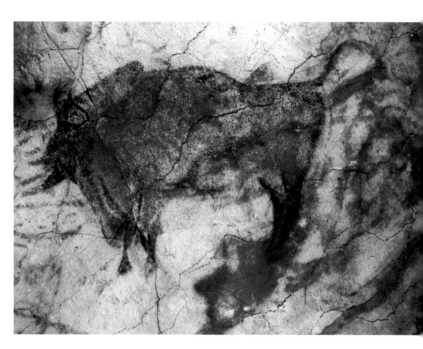

A 16,000-year-old painting of a large male bison on the ceiling of the Altamira cave in northern Spain. Some archaeologists have speculated that Solutrean people, who created Europe's prehistoric cave paintings, may have migrated to North America.

not really pioneers but rather descendants of a long line of forebears who had been learning to live in the New World of the Americas for thousands of years. Many researchers now agree that Stone Age immigrants arrived in the Americas between 20,000 and 30,000 years ago. They came at different times and from different parts of the globe—certainly from Asia, and perhaps also from Europe, Africa, and Australia, traveling by land and by sea—and over the millennia they spread across the virgin lands of the New World.

Meanwhile, researchers continue to make fresh discoveries about how and when the New World was first populated. Recently uncovered sites along the Savannah River in South Carolina and at Pedra Furada in Brazil hint that migrants may have been coming to the Americas for as long as 50,000 years—far earlier than any previously known human presence. "You couldn't have a more exciting time to be involved in the whole issue of the peopling of the Americas," says University of Texas archaeologist Michael Collins. "Surprising new finds keep rocking the boat and launching fresh waves of debate."

Perhaps one day soon, somewhere in the Americas, someone walking across a field will discover a surprising new clue—an ancient stone tool made with care and left in that very spot by a human being who was alive once. Behind that ancient stone tool will be a hand reaching out of the past and taking ours.

A Clovis spear point found at an archaeological dig near Woodward, Oklahoma, on July 3, 2002.

CHAPTER NOTES

The following notes refer to the sources of quoted material within the text. Each citation includes the first and last words or phrases of the quotation and the source. Unless otherwise noted, references are to works cited in the Selected Bibliography, starting on page 83.

Abbreviations used are:

Church—Sally K. Church, *Monumenta Serica 53*
Davies—Nigel Davies, *The Ancient Kingdoms of Mexico*
Finlay—Robert Finlay, *Journal of World History*
Fitzhugh—William W. Fitzhugh, *Vikings*
Ingstad—Helge Ingstad, *The Viking Discovery of America*
Josephy—Alvin M. Josephy Jr., *America in 1492*
Levathes—Louise Levathes, *When China Ruled the Seas*
Lewis—Brenda Ralph Lewis, *The Aztecs*
Log—Robert H. Fuson, *The Log of Christopher Columbus*
Mann—Charles C. Mann, *1491*
Menzies—Gavin Menzies, *1421*
Rozario—Paul Rozario, *Zheng He and the Treasure Fleet*
Sagas—Magnus Magnusson, *The Vinland Sagas*
Thomas—Hugh Thomas, *Rivers of Gold*

CHAPTER ONE: ADMIRAL OF THE OCEAN SEA

Page
2–3   "I am having . . . some night": Log, September 24, 1492, p. 66
6   "There is no . . . half the earth": Thomas, p. 55
8   "the grandeurs . . . universe": Thomas, p. 74
11   "They are . . . paunch": Log, October 12, p. 76
    "because all . . . vicinity": Log, October 24, p. 92
12   "that might . . . leave here": Log, October 21, p. 89
    "They gave . . . they had": Log, December 19, p. 134
    "They brought . . . wonderful": Log, December 21, p. 144

13   "They are . . . smiling": Log, December 25, p. 153
    "the sand . . . *del Oro*": Log, January 8, 1493, p. 168
14   "there were tears . . . eyes": Thomas, p. 105
15   "good sample . . . parrots": Thomas, p. 164
16–17   "Bobadilla . . . why": Thomas, p. 197
17   "I have seen . . . gold": Thomas, p. 483

CHAPTER TWO: DID CHINA DISCOVER AMERICA?

20   *Let the dark . . . correct route*: Levathes, pp. 31–32
23   "lofty and majestic . . . gigantic": Church, p. 13
24   "as loud . . . bell": Rozario, p. 34
    "sparkled like . . . river": Levathes, p. 87
25   "I have seen . . . sky": Levathes, p. 40
30   "master chart . . . world": "Goodbye, Columbus!" by Jack Hitt, *New York Times,* January 5, 2003
31   "a buried object . . . Chinese origin": Menzies, p. 242
    "may be . . . hurricane": Menzies, p. 316
31   "It is more . . . Chinese": Menzies, p. 333
31–32   "striking resemblance": Menzies, p. 331
33   "whatever message . . . read": Menzies, p. 336
    "A chain . . . quality": "Gavin Menzies: What Historians at the AHA Made of His Claim That the Chinese Discovered America," by Ken Ringle, *Washington Post,* January 12, 2004
33   "obsessed amateur," ibid.
34   "almost every . . . destroyed": Menzies, p. 35
    "those few . . . survived": Menzies, p. 111
    "the missing years": Menzies, p. 111
    "There are plentiful . . . 'missing years'": Finlay, p. 3 of downloaded version
    "The voyages . . . never took place": Finlay, p. 7 of downloaded version
35   "The evidence . . . day": "Goodbye, Columbus!" by Jack Hitt, *New York Times,* January 5, 2003
36   "Most scholars . . . 1000 B.C.": Levathes, p. 28

37   "strong indications . . . South America": Levathes, p. 25

"The Chinese . . . contact": Levathes, p. 22

38   "a strong influx . . . elements": Levathes, p. 40

"Some outside . . . seafarers": Levathes, p. 40

CHAPTER THREE: LEIF THE LUCKY

43   "Yes . . . houses": "Helge Ingstad, 101, Discoverer of Viking Site," obituary in *Halifax Sunday Herald,* April 1, 2001

43–44 "The excavations . . . long ago": Ingstad, pp. 135–36

50   "tall and strong . . . behavior": Sagas, p. 56

53   "In the spring . . . grapes": Sagas, pp. 57–58

55   "a rich . . . inhabit": Fitzhugh, p. 193

CHAPTER FOUR: THE NOT-SO-NEW WORLD

58   "a bee hive . . . countries": Mann, p. 132

58   "thickly set . . . from one": Mann, p. 98

61   "such absolute . . . territories": "The Founding Sachems," by Charles C. Mann, *New York Times,* July 4, 2005

64   "to whom . . . advantageous": *Benjamin Franklin,* by Edmund S. Morgan (New Haven: Yale University Press, 2002), p. 80

64   "None of . . . reverence": Davies, p. 190

65–66 "We were . . . dream": Lewis, p. xiii

66   "Our heritage . . . down": Josephy, p. 175

CHAPTER FIVE: WHO REALLY DISCOVERED AMERICA?

80   "These were . . . similar solutions": "America's First Immigrants," by Evan Hadingham, *Smithsonian Magazine,* November 2004, p. 96

"The actual point . . . New World": ibid., p. 98

81   "You couldn't . . . debate": ibid., p. 91

SELECTED BIBLIOGRAPHY

CHAPTER ONE: ADMIRAL OF THE OCEAN SEA

The log kept by Christopher Columbus during his first voyage to the New World, available in several versions and translations, is an essential primary source for any student of that historic expedition. While Columbus's judgments on arriving in the West Indies are inevitably colored by his cultural bias and his need to please his royal sponsors, his first impressions are often immediate and fresh. I quote from *The Log of Christopher Columbus,* translated by Robert H. Fuson (Camden, Me.: International Marine Publishing Co., 1987).

Among recent biographies of Columbus, *The Worlds of Christopher Columbus,* by William D. Phillips Jr. and Carla Rahn Phillips (New York: Cambridge University Press, 1992) is a highly regarded work for both the specialist and the general reader. *Admiral of the Ocean Sea,* by Samuel Eliot Morison (New York: Little, Brown and Company, reissue edition 1991), won the Pulitzer Prize for biography in 1942 and was long considered the definitive life of Columbus.

For events surrounding Columbus's voyage, I drew on the magisterial *Rivers of Gold: The Rise of the Spanish Empire from Columbus to Magellan,* by Hugh Thomas (New York: Random House, 2003). My account of the Tainos, their culture, and their fate was informed by *The Tainos: Rise and Decline of the People Who Greeted Columbus,* by Irving Rouse (New Haven: Yale University Press, 1992), and *The Art of the Taino from the Dominican Republic,* by John F. Scott (Gainesville, Fla.: University Presses of Florida, 1985).

CHAPTER TWO:
DID CHINA DISCOVER AMERICA?

The book that suggested this chapter is the controversial best-seller *1421: The Year China Discovered America,* by Gavin Menzies (New York: William Morrow, 2003). A probing PBS documentary based on the book, *1421: The Year China Discovered America?,* added a question mark to the title. It is available as a PBS home video (FYCA601).

The authoritative *When China Ruled the Seas: The Treasure Fleet of the Dragon Throne, 1405–1433,* by Louise Levathes (New York: Oxford University Press, 1994), discusses the documented voyages of Zheng He's treasure fleet as far as East Africa and scholarly speculation that Chinese voyagers may have reached the Americas centuries before 1421. *Zheng He and the Treasure Fleet, 1405–1433: A Modern-Day Traveller's Guide from Antiquity to the Present,* by Paul Rozario (Singapore: SNP International, 2005), is a lavishly illustrated account of the Ming Dynasty exploration and trade fleets.

Two scholarly articles were particularly informative: "Zheng He: An Investigation into the Plausibility of 450-foot Treasure Ships," by Sally K. Church, published online by *Monumenta Serica* 53 (2005), 1–43, and "How Not to (Re)Write World History: Gavin Menzies and the Chinese Discovery of America," by Robert Finlay, *Journal of World History,* June 1, 2004.

Several websites, both supporting and debunking Gavin Menzies's theories, can be accessed at Google by entering: "1421—The Year China Discovered America."

CHAPTER THREE: LEIF THE LUCKY

The Vikings' territorial expansion from their Scandinavian homeland across the Atlantic to North America a thousand years ago was the subject of a major exhibition in 2000 at the Smithsonian's National Museum of Natural History, and later at major cities in North America. The companion volume to the exhibition, *Vikings: The North Atlantic Saga,* edited by William W. Fitzhugh and Elisabeth I. Ward (Washington, D.C.: Smithsonian Institution Press, 2000), includes 31 articles by leading scholars in an array of fields and over five hundred illustrations and maps.

The Viking Discovery of America: The Excavation of a Norse Settlement in L'Anse aux Meadows, Newfoundland, by Helge Ingstad and Anne Stine Ingstad (New York: Checkmark Books, 2001), offers a first-hand account by the archaeologists who discovered and researched the Viking site. *Full Circle—First Contact: Vikings and Skraelings in Newfoundland and Labrador,* edited by Kevin E. McAleese (St. John's, Nfl.: Newfoundland Museum, 2000), is the informative companion volume to a traveling exhibit sponsored by the Newfoundland Museum and the Government of Newfoundland and Labrador.

The Oxford Illustrated History of the Vikings, edited by Peter Sawyer (Oxford and New York: Oxford University Press, 1997), is an excellent general history with contributions by ten scholars.

My references to the Vinland sagas are from *The Vinland Sagas: The Norse Discovery of America,* translated with an introduction by Magnus Magnusson and Herman Pálsson (Baltimore: Penguin Books, 1965).

CHAPTER FOUR: THE NOT-SO-NEW-WORLD

1491: New Revelations of the Americas Before Columbus, by Charles C. Mann (New York: Alfred A. Knopf, 2005), an engrossing and myth-shattering book, presents a sweeping survey of human life in the Americas before the European invasion, from the earliest prehistoric settlers to the Pilgrims' first encounter with the Indians. *America in 1492: The World of the Indian Peoples Before the Arrival of Columbus,* edited by Alvin M. Josephy Jr. (New York: Alfred A. Knopf, 1992), approaches the same subject through essays by sixteen contributors.

Other sources for this chapter include *The Penguin History of Latin America,* by Edwin Williamson (London and New York: Penguin Books, 1992); *The Ancient Kingdoms of Mexico,* by Nigel Davies (New York: Penguin Books, 1982); and *The Aztecs,* by Brenda Ralph Lewis (Phoenix Mill–Thrupp–Stroud–Gloucestershire: Sutton Publishing, 1999).

CHAPTER FIVE:
WHO REALLY DISCOVERED AMERICA?

Charles C. Mann's book, cited above, was a valuable source for this chapter. Other recent books on early human migrations include *Before the Dawn: Recovering the Lost History of Our Ancestors,* by Nicholas Wade (New York: Penguin Press, 2006); *New Perspectives on the First Americans,* edited by Bradley T. Lepper and Robson Bonnichsen (College Station, Tex.: Texas A & M University Press: Center for the Study of the First Americans, 2004); *The First Americans: In Pursuit of Archaeology's Greatest Mystery,* by J. M. Adovasio (New York: Random House, 2002); *In Search of Ice Age Americans,* by Kenneth B. Tankersley (Salt Lake City: Gibbs Smith, 2002); and *The Settlement of the Americas: A New Prehistory,* by Thomas D. Dillehay (New York: Basic Books, 2000).

Recent archaeological discoveries, along with a flood of new research findings in genetics and linguistics, are constantly altering interpretations of the historical record and fueling the debate about the origins of the first Americans. Much of the material for this chapter came from recent newspaper and magazine articles, among them "America's First Immigrants" by Evan Hadingham, *Smithsonian Magazine,* November 2004; "Who Were the First Americans?" by Michael D. Lemonick and Andrea Dorfman, *Time* magazine, March 13, 2006; and a transcript of the *Nova* television special "America's Stone Age Explorers," which aired on PBS November 9, 2004.

Websites for virtually every subject touched upon in this book, from "Christopher Columbus" to "Prehistoric Migrations to the Americas," can be accessed through *Google*.

ACKNOWLEDGMENTS AND PICTURE CREDITS

I am grateful to the following people for their generous assistance and advice while I researched this book:

Jacquelyn Cavis, Curator of Art, Ventura County Maritime Museum; Dr. Sally K. Church, Wolfson College, Cambridge University; Loretta Decker, Historic Site Supervisor, L'Anse aux Meadows National Historic Site; Charlotte Houtz, Geography and Map Division, Library of Congress; Kevin E. McAleese, Curatorial Team Chairperson, Newfoundland Museum; Lynda Unchern, Cambridge University Library Imaging Services.

Illustrations courtesy of:

American Museum of Natural History: 65, 69, 73, 77
AP/Wide World Photos: 36, 56, 58, 66, 70, 71, 74, 76, 80, 81
Bettmann/CORBIS: 42
Gianni Dagli/CORBIS: 72
Mary Evans Picture Library: vi–vii, 41, 45, 55

Library of Congress: viii, 4, 5, 7, 14, 16, 19, 28–29, 31, 48, 49, 64, 68
The Newberry Library: 59, 60, 67
General Research Division, The New York Public Library, Astor, Lenox, and Tilden Foundations: 12, 13
Picture Collection, The Branch Libraries, The New York Public Library, Astor, Lenox, and Tilden Foundations: frontispiece, 9, 40, 62
Rare Books Division, The New York Public Library, Astor, Lenox, and Tilden Foundations: 18
Tu, Shen, The Tribute Giraffe with Attendant, Philadelphia Museum of Art: Gift of John T. Dorrance, 1977: 25
The Rooms, Provincial Museum Division, St. John's, Newfoundland: 52
The Rooms, Provincial Museum Division/Parks Canada: 53 (top)
Ventura County Maritime Museum: 21, 22
Photos on pages 50, 51, and 53 (bottom) were taken by the author

INDEX

Note: Page numbers in *italic* type refer to illustrations.